Teacher Certification Exam

# Home Economics

## Written By:

Barbara Teman,  B.S.

**To Order Additional Copies:**
Xam, Inc.
99 Central St.
Worcester, MA 01605
Toll Free     1-800-301-4647
Phone:        1-508 363 0633
Email:        winwin1111@aol.com
Web           www.xamonline.com
EFax          1-501-325-0185
Fax:          1-508-363-0634

**You will find:**
- Content Review in prose format
- Bibliography
- Sample Test

## XAM, INC.
*Building Better Teachers*

D1501794

"And, while there's no reason yet to panic, I think it's only prudent that we make preperations to panic."

CST: Home Economics
ISBN: 1-58197-141-9

## DEDICATION

I would like to dedicate this study guide to my parents, Frieda and Louis Glantz for insisting on my getting a College degree. Also I must dedicate this book to my dad, Sidney Glantz who taught me to go on no matter what the obstacle. I want my in-laws to know they have helped raise me to and I appreciate all their efforts. Without all my families help I couldn't have finished this study guide. So I dedicate this entire book to my loving husband, Stuart, and my two sons, Mychal and Jason Teman. They are my true pride and joys.

"Mrs. Hammond, I'd know you anywhere from little Billy's portrait of you."

## TABLE OF COMPETENCIES AND SKILLS, PERCENTAGES, AND REVIEW SOURCES

There are explanations of each competency and/or skill. Please use this information as a study guide like cliff notes when preparing for the certification test.

**COMPETENCY/SKILL**                                               **4.1%**

**COMPETENCY 1.0    PERSONALITY DEVELOPMENT INFORMATION**

### SKILL 1.1    What heredity factors help or hurt ones growth and development?

Being born with a calm patient dispositition makes for an easier life. If your parents give you a trait of being high strung or oversensitive, lifes daily situations will be more stressful. Genetics plays a large part in the offsprings looks and growth.

### SKILL 1.2    What environmental factors promote or harm individual growth and development?

The status or class you are raised in influences your development greatly. Whether you are part of the upper, middle, or lower economic class, will determine your environment. Your life will be controlled by your status in the economic hierachy.

### SKILL 1.3    Maslow's Basic Needs

Maslow believes people grow in a pyramid of both physical and emotional needs. Body needs must be satisfied before a person can advance and grow. They are at the bottom of the pyramid. If hunger and sleep are satisfied you move up to a comfort stage. That's no stress. Next is the need for love. The next level is getting respect or building your self-esteem. At the top is when a person has reached all their goals. They are fully satisfied in life. Maslow thinks only 40% of adults get to the top of the hierarchy.

### SKILL 1.4    What is self-esteem?

Self-esteem is the way one sees their own worth. It's a feeling of satisfaction about ones self. Hopefully it is a high opinion of ones capabilities. Those with high self-esteem tend to do better at whatever they try while those with low self-esteem seem to do poorly at new things. The best thing to improve ones self-esteem is to begin with small successes and move up to greater successes . Self-esteem is how you view yourself. If you have high self-esteem with confidence you achieve more. The opposite is true as well. If you think very little of yourself, you won't achieve much.

## SKILL 1.5  Identify Ways to Improve Self-esteem.

The best way to raise self-esteem is with each new success.  These achievements whether big or small are the way to a better self-esteem.  Another way is a life review.  You simply think of your past experiences.  This way you can put  some order to those various experiences.  You can see your old previous successes.  These two ways can help anyone improve their self-esteem.

## SKILL 1.6  Self-esteem is molded  by your family.

As a baby you see several role models like your mom and dad.  As you perform both parents oooo and aaaa.  This builds up your self-esteem.  As you walk mom and dad cheer.  All these experiences feed into your self-esteem.  On the other hand if a child grows up with abuse, low self-esteem would be the result.  This proves that how and what  parents do for  or with their children will control the child's future self-esteem.

## SKILL 1.7  Without a positive self-concept one can never reach Maslow's level of self-actualization.

First your basic needs like hunger or sleep are satisfied.  Next  your safety needs are taken care of.  The third level fills your need of love and belonging.  The fourth level requires that a high self-esteem must be reached.  If one has low self-esteem he won't care to even try to attain any  type of success.  The need for self-actualization comes only if all four types  of deficiencies are corrected.

## SKILL 1.8  What influences  the development of a positive  outlook.

Again  having, normal parents as role models that have high self-esteem is a plus.  Having  a positive mental attitude can help keep you  healthy.  Your immune system  picks up  on your state of mind and works better if you are in a positive frame of mind.

## SKILL 1.9  What factors help one understand their sexuality?

Age effects your sex role.  As a child boys and girls are not far apart.After marriage and with children the women must nurture.  Now the men are different sexually than the mother. They  worry  about  the  money. All  previous experiences influences sexuality. Sex roles influence peoples decisions at crucial times in your life.

## SKILL 1.10  What factors of personality development  make one different?

Personality is ones method of relating to the environment.  It is  your temperment.  Temperment is your emotional response to a stimuli.  People are consistent in personality.  If shy at 10 and at 40 then still shy at 65.  Maturity effects your personality.

## SKILL 1.11 Personality development is influenced by your relations with peers, family, or adults.

Who you grow up with usually are your role models. If the role models show positive personality traits the children will copy these. The relationship between children and parents continue throughout life. These relationships are very strong and influence among peers, family, and adults.

**HOME ECONOMICS**

## COMPETENCY 2.0 DECISION-MAKING/PROBLEM SOLVING     31%

### SKILL 2. 1  Values and Self-development

Values are formed early in life when you were a child seeing your parents life problems. Using the 5 steps in decision-making always works as a problem solving system.

    identify the problems
    list the alternatives
C. pick a plan
D. Do it
E. Evaluate the results

Your self-development will take on a healthy direction. If you are in an atmosphere of positive personalities. Your values are what you feel is important. These things will be protected by you.

## COMPETENCY 3.0     COMMUNICATION SKILLS     2%

### SKILL 3.1 Various communication skills

Exchanging information between two individuals in communication. That can be verbal or with body language. Use accurate and honest information. Giving positive feedback helps with good communication. If you need to tell your partner that his behavior is bothering you . Do it in a positive manner. Using "I: messages helps you let your partner know something is bothering you without putting your partner down.. The process of how the message is given will determine the flow it will take to the partner.

## COMPETENCY 4.0    MARRIAGE PREPARATION

### SKILL 4.1  Preparing for Marriage
Commitment to a partner for love, support, and differences,
Those planning to marry need a blood test.  Consider the cost of a wedding.
The honeymoon is a rite of privacy for the bride and the groom.  Marriage will
effect your relationships with parents and friends.  Everyone will be secondary
too your spouse.

### SKILL 4.2  With marriage each partner has many roles that effect the relationships.
Married  people have more regular hours than singles out looking for  a
partner. Mates try to make each other happy. All other relationships like with
your mother, father, brother, or sister will change because now it will be effected
by the spouse.  Each partner will try to fulfill their mates intellectual, physical,
and emotional needs.  This is not realistic.  But to try to satisfy your  partners
needs is admirable.  Marriage causes the newlyweds to see their parents less.
Friends are seen less.

### SKILL 4.3  If husband and wife are  both employed how does this effect the home, and  husband, family?
There are a  few obstacles for  the wife.   They are children. The  wife always
makes the childcare arrangements.  More domestic responsibilities rest with the
wife.  Even if she has a full time career, she still  does 90% of  the housework.
This can get    exhausting.  In a study done in 1982, 100 marriages of dual-
careers were looked at.  These couples turned out  to be more educated, had
higher incomes, were younger, were children or had fewer children.

### SKILL  4.4 What are the dual roles and responsibilities of the spouses in a relationship?
The wife again takes care of   the childcare arrangements.  It's as if someone
else is raising  the children Yet they are taken care of.  They are away from else
is  raising  the children.  Yet they are taken care of.  They are away from the
house from about 8a.m.-7p.m..  Does all that fast food or frozen foods harm the
families? This wives proud how she juggles family, house,  career, and  spouse.
The  husband need only support the wives  career.  He then needs to help with
the children.  He can do housework too.  Any loving spouse will come around
and be  helpful to the wife.

### SKILL 4.5  Laws and customs of Marriage

Thirteen states recognize common law marriage.  Marriage is a stable force where children are  raised.   Usually though couples have a ceremony.  The friends bring gifts to help  the couple get a good start.   There are  3 types of marriage: monogamy ,polygamy, and  group marriages.  Monogamy is with   1 wife and 1 husband.  This is the only  legal marriage in the United States.  Polygamy is where there are several spouses, like one man with 3 wives.  This is not legal in the United States.  This type of marriage is popular in Africa.

### SKILL 4.6  Preparing a Marriage with customs and ceremonies.  The first step is commitment.  This separates your spouse from all you know.  The spouse is now  your one and only.  But now you are committed to your spouses family  also.  Next you become legally bound at a ceremony called the wedding.  This wedding is a rite of passage.  Blood tests are often required of  the happy couple The marriage license is issued at the county courthouse.   A strong custom is that the bride wear something old, new, borrowed, and blue to the ceremony.  The bride later throws out her bouquet to be caught by a single girl.

## COMPETENCY 5.0  MARITAL STABILITY                    3.1%

### SKILL 5.1  A stable marital relationship

To have a stable marriage, you must be ready to work at it.  After marriage there will be changes.  Personal changes may build up  your  self-concept.  Or you mat get depressed in your new situation.  A happy medium must be reached.  You may have imagined how it would be when  you got  married and it isn't.  To reach stability you need   to talk to your spouse.  Fifty per cent of all marriages end in divorce.  But then 60% get remarried.  You also know no one can fill all of another person's needs.  Allow your spouse the  freedom of other friendships.  Relationships with friends loose their appeal.  But keep up on them.  Everyone   needs friends.  Sexually your   experimenting   on pleasing your spouse.  More women than men do housework.  Get your spouse to help you with normal chores.  There may be  financial matters to work out.  Most of all remain open to communication with your spouse.  This is the only way to a successful marriage.

### SKILL 5.2  Factors in Marriage to Adjust to.

Open communication is vital to a healthy marriage.  Consider your  finances as a couple.  Set up  workable budget.  Housework needs to be divided up  so   that the wife isn't stuck with 90% of the chores.  Keep your friends involved in your life.  Get your parents and spouses to get along.  Work out the dual career arrangements together.  Like check on   daycares together.   Both parents interview nighttime baby-sitters.  Sex may   be an issue,  This too can be resolved with   open communication between spouses.  If there are different religions, races, or age problems.  The partners must work hard to make it work.

### SKILL 5.3  Adjustment to Marriage

Again only with open  communication can any couple work out a problem.  If it's sex,  money, fun, food, or family, it all has to be worked out for the family to survive.  One method to adjust is with a total separation.  The  two meet without interruptions too discuss the problem.   Only when it's solved can the quarantine be lifted.  Arrange for children to be cared for  somewhere else.  Marriage involves personal, social, and legal charges for the spouses.

**COMPETENCY 6.0       PREPARING FOR PARENTHOOD       2.1%**

### SKILL 6.1  Readiness for Parenthood.

You must be selfless as a parent.  All parents shower their children with material gifts.  Yet they expect a thanks.  Forget it.  Most children expect material gifts.  Read Theories of Childbearing by Gesell.  This will point out what's expected by a baby at different developmental stages.  Using a reward, not a punishment  is one way to alter a child's behavior.  Give a cookie each time you leave and the child doesn't cry.  Parent effectiveness training is a terrific way to get ready to have a child.  This may be  offered at  your  local high school.  Active listening is good for childbearing.  You must  truely hear what your child says.  Time must be spent with the parents and the children.

### SKILL 6.2  What are the Responsibilities for Parenthood.

It all begins with  planning.  Figuring  how many children do you want?  How much space do you want between them?  Don't have too many children.  If you can't clothe and feed them easily.

### SKILL 6.3  Discuss economical, physical, and psychological  results for a family deciding on a child or not.

Children cost money.   One child costs $133,000 up to 18 years old. Physically another body makes  the house more crowded.  Psychologically there is competition for the parents attention among siblings.  When the woman is ready to go back to work, she has so much to get  ready to  take a child to daycare.  Families with children will go out much less.

### SKILL 6.4  Preparental Responsibilities for Parenthood are liking children.

You need to be happily married.  You  realize having a family to care for takes allot of time.  You and your spouse will have less time just for the two of you.  If you have Tasachs or an inheritable disease you must tell your spouse before you get pregnant.  Are you a caring person?  You need to be to  care for an infant.

### SKILL 6.5  Prepare for the Baby

Stay close throughout the pregnancy.  Make a nursery.  Arrange for Lamaze lessons.  Read parenting books.  Set aside any extra money.  Babies are expensive.  Motherhood brings many emotions to the surface.  She has a whole new set of responsibilities.  Fathers will help with the new born if guided into this gently.

## SKILL 6.6 Male and Female Reproductive Systems

The female reproductive system starts with a release of the egg, ova, from the fallopian tubes where a male sperm swims up and penetrates the egg shell or fertilized it. It hooks on to the lining. Here it will grow. The male reproductive system provides the sperm to fertilize. The sperm are made in the seminal vesicles.

## SKILL 6.7 Family Planning

To be successful at family planning is to have the number of children you wanted and spaced how you want them. When considering family planning you spaced how you wanted them. How many? When? and What type of birth control to use until baby time. Babies cost about $5,774 the first year. Society encourages families, one generation to another to continue. Many friends with children are pushing the childless couples to get busy and have some babies. Religions are pro family expansion. The United States government supports parenthood too.

## SKILL 6.8 Does Family Planning effect economic, social, and intellectual development of people and families?

Of course family planning effects economics. Another family member means more money spent on food, clothes, and diapers. Socially more children calls or more get together for celebration . So socially we're all better off. The families must nurture the new babies intellect. Exposure is a must for babies. They learn so quickly.

## SKILL 6.9 Birth control

Birth control is used to avoid getting pregnant. There's many usable methods. Examples are the pill, the condom, the IUD, a diaphragm, or gels. The birth control pill contains hormones estrogen and progesterone. It won't allow the sperm in. . The complication is blood clots and high blood pressure. Women over 40 are at risk of high blood pressure. Women over 40 are at risk if on the pill. Many women on birth control suffered from nausea, weight gain, breast tenderness, control pills find them very convenient. Many women on the pill have side effects. They may suffer from nausea, weight gain, breast tenderness, headaches, and moodswings. Yet birth control pills are very convenient. A condom is a safe birth control means. Be careful when removing a used one after intercourse. Now dispose of it. The condom also protects the male from sexually transmitted diseases. The female can use an IUD to stop pregnancy. A doctor must insert the IUD. There's two popular types, the copper or the Progesterone. People with IUD's experience side effects like cramps and heavier periods. With the diaphragm you must use a spermicide. Or use a foam or a gel. There is a vaginal sponge now on the market. It's 2" and filled with spermicide. Today is the name at the drugstore.

The sponge is put in the vagina. But it can not be used during menstruation. There is the rhythm or calendar method. Take your temperature each morning. It goes down when you ovulate. On the day you ovulate withdrawal is a poor method. Douching right after intercourse sometimes stops pregnancy. There is a morning after pill called DES. Also 486 will end the morning after pill, called DES. Also the 486 will end a pregnancy. But if babies are planned for, they'll be a bundle of joy.

## SKILL 6.10 Responsibilities of Parenting

You need to be stable economically, emotionally and as one entity. If you both work set up a budget. Put so much in the bank for yourself. Pay your bills together. Neither should be in the dark on how much it costs for you to have you lifestyle. If you have a baby, who 's going to stay home? Are you both strong enough for an addition to the family? It will mean extra chores. A lot more pressures. If you are like one, having a new little guy in the family can be just terrific.

## COMPETENCY 7.0 PRENATAL CARE, DEVELOPMENT, AND CHILDBIRTH.          4.1%

### SKILL 7.1 Terms of Pregnancy

Fertilization takes place now she is pregnant. The ova and the sperm become a zygote. They hook onto the wall of the uterus. As the cells divide the baby becomes an embryo. The baby will develop in the mother for nine months. When one is pregnant they must eat right. It's important to see your doctor to get vitamins. You'll finally feel the baby move around in the fifth month of the pregnancy.

### SKILL 7.2 Fetus Development

What the mother eats feeds the baby. The mother should take a vitamin recommended by the doctor. The young pregnant lady needs to exercise. Bike riding or swimming are excellent examples. She has to sleep at night about eight hours. During the day she needs to rest too. No reaching up over her head. Think. When eating right, try small portions. Breakfast could be a bowl of cereal and milk and orange juice. Lunch could be yogurt and crackers plus a salad. For dinner try three ounces of a lean meat with green beans, and a baked potato A salad before dinner is fine.

### SKILL 7.3 Prenatal Care and Needs of an Expectant Mother.

The mother to be needs much rest to prepare for the birth. She must be eating right and taking her vitamins. The baby needs to be bathed, given bottles of formula , and coddled allot. The baby is so helpless to begin with. The mother may take sitz baths after delivery. She'll pop back into shape before no time. Because the baby will cry in the middle of the night for a bottle it's nice to have a rocking chair, couch, or bed at which you can nurse the little new addition. It's helpful to get help in the house the first week that the infant comes home from the hospital. For instance your mother or mother-in-law.

### SKILL 7.4 Exercise and rest during pregnancy.

I've already mentioned the importance for proper care of a pregnant woman. She must follow her doctor's care. That would include a balanced diet of three meals with snacks daily. She should take vitamins prescribed from the doctor. She must exercise like walking or swimming. Have six to eight glasses of water daily. Sleep eight hours nightly. Rest during the day. The pregnant woman must simply relax because she will be so busy when the baby arrives.

### SKILL 7.5  Diet for a pregnant woman

The food pyramid should be followed daily. This is a lowfat, low protein, high carbohydrate formula. Drink 8 eight-ounce glasses of water too. A program like weight watchers fits the guidelines of the American Heart Association which is recommended to follow for good health Use oil, sugars, salts, and fats sparingly. Have four dairy servings daily. Have two 3 ounces per serving of meat. Have 3-5 vegetables and 3-4 fruits daily too. You need 6-11 grains. This describes the food guide pyramid. Use it.

### SKILL 7.6  Complications Of Pregnancy

Many different things can happen during the pregnancy. The baby may be in the position to come out of mom feet first which is very difficult. The baby's blood may not blend with the mother's blood. At birth there will be transfusions necessary. This is known as a blue baby. There are many more problems that could harm the mother like toxemia. That's where your body holds all liquids. Usually the ankles, wrist, and face puff or swell up. This is dangerous for the baby too. Simply see your doctor on time and take care of yourself and the baby.

### SKILL 7.7  Pregnancies of Adolescents and older Women.

Teenager pregnancy is usually accompanied by dropping out of school and low birth weight. There are 1,000,000 teenagers having babies in the United States in a year. About half elect abortion. There's a higher number than teens in many European countries. As for older women having babies, the chance of Down Syndrome is more probable. The delivery may be too tough for the older mother. Older pregnant moms get toxemia more often too.

### SKILL 7.8  Labor and Delivery

Labor begins with cramps. They get more intense and come closer together. There's three stages. First your cervix will dilate to ten centimeters. Your lining is effacing or pulling back. The birth canal is ready. When the water breaks in the ammniotic sac, labor will move faster into the next phase. The baby is coming down the birth canal. When the transition stage starts the mom's mood will swing. At this point the contractions are very close. All are in place. Third stage the baby's head crowns(first shows). Next the baby slips out. The mom puffed and worked so hard. When she first sees the baby,she forgets all the pain. One last step is the afterbirth which was when the ammonitic sac came out. The baby is weighed, cleaned, and wrapped up by the nurse.

**HOME ECONOMICS**

### SKILL 7.9  Delivery Types

There are four well known methods of birth widely used in the United States. They are Lamaze, Dick-Read, Bradlry, LeBoyer, and Cesarean births.

Lamaze is often called 'natural' childbirth. It was developed in France. The woman and spouse go to childbirth classes to reduce anxiety over the birth of their baby. You learn about labor and delivery. You learn and practice breathing exercises for delivery. Also relaxation and pain control exercises are learned by the mom to be. Of course the husband is the coach. He guides the wife through the breathing exercises.

With the Dick-Read method we try to stop the pregnant person from being afraid. This was achieved with breathing and relaxation exercises. The husband also remains supportive throughout the delivery of their child. With the Bradley method it attained the name the "husband coached" childbirth. It is similar to Lamaze.

LeBoyer method is named for the French founder. Low lit delivery room. Baby placed on the mother's belly right after birth. Then the baby is placed in warm water to relax. Next the nurse wraps up the baby nice and warm.

These are drug free means of delivery. There is also the caudal or epidural, which is anesthesia. There is cesarean births which are used if there is a risk to the mom or the baby. An incision is made in the mom's abdomen. The woman is put to sleep with anesthesia. The baby is removed from the abdomen. If it were a breech birth with a chance of the umbilical cord wrapping around the infant's neck.

### SKILL 7.10  A Healthy Newborn Baby

Your DNA or chromosomes determine your looks, sex, and emotions. A normal baby has 44 regular chromosomes. Hormones develop your sexual being. There will be 10 toes and ten fingers. The legs and arms are often pulled into the baby's center in the fetal position. This is for security and warmth. The liver is the largest organ in the child at birth. It may not even start functioning right away. The condition know as jaundice has entered the child. He or she will appear yellow in the eyeballs and possibly the skin will look yellowish. Then too much iron is in the baby's system. See the pediatrician right away. The skin is pasty or dry and needs lotion. There may be some head hair to use baby no tear shampoo on. Watch out for the softspot at the top of the head . The skull or cranial bones are not fused together at birth. This leaves the precious brain unprotected. It closes up during the first year of life. The eyes are extremely clear just after birth. The nurse puts silver nitrate drops in the eyes for syphilis. Now the eyes get puffy and red. Too bad this is a necessary precaution. The baby may have little fingernails that require careful cutting. Otherwise the baby will scratch themselves. The umbylical cord dries up. It turns brown like a scab and falls off a few weeks after delivery. Frequent diaper changes are important for
the average seven pound baby that's 21 inches long.

## SKILL 7.11 Postnatal Care of Mother and Baby

At first all new mothers feel elated. Then depression, crying, and difficulty in sleeping can start . These mom's need help from dad or parents. Some may even need therapy. If a new mom can get help with the family chores and laundry, she can focus on the newborn alone. This is a better bonding regimen because mom relaxed. Baby needs an insurmountable amount of attention. Mom and relatives will help here. Mom needs to see her doctor at six weeks after delivery. Again she should be eating right, exercising a little, and drinking 6-8 glasses of water each day. The baby needs to see the pediatrician at one month. If anything looks out of the ordinary with the baby call the doctor immediately.

## SKILL 7.12 Birth Defects

Women that get pregnant after 40 must be concerned about Down's Syndrome. Down's Syndrome produces slow children. The nose bridge is flattened. The eyes slant and are far apart. These other conditions are possible birth defects, achondroplasia ,Marfan Syndrome, apert syndrome, and bony growths.

## SKILL 7.13 Prenatal Care Prevents Birth Defects

If the mother is attentive to her needs during pregnancy she will produce a healthy baby. If the young mother-to-be goes to her doctor and follows his directions there should be no problems. Eat right following the food guide pyramid. Get a little exercise daily like walking or swimming. Get eight hours of sleep and rest during the day. Be sure to take a multiple vitamin. Relaxation during pregnancy is vital. After birth the new mother will be busy. By taking special care for the pregnant one you are helping the baby get strong too. If you take care of yourself the birth defects are pushed away from the baby.

HOME ECONOMICS

## COMPETENCY 8.0  SOCIAL, EMOTIONAL, PHYSICAL,  AND INTELLECTUAL DEVELOPMENT
4.1%

### SKILL 8.1  How chromosomes form your heredity

Each person ends up with 44 chromosomes plus two sex chromosomes.  An XX is a girl, one from each parent.  A XY combination designates a boy.  Now the zygote is an embryo.  The hormones help the reproductive system organs to be formed.  Once born the baby grows fast.  By one they walk and by two they talk.  Babies aren't interested in socializing.  They usually are me oriented, in other words babies like all  the attention they get.  Between one and two they should be taught to use the potty.  Diapers are expensive.  Couples need to quit using them as soon as possible.  The baby crawls early.  The baby can chase a ball at 6 months. Near two a small big wheel bike can be controlled.  Motor development is a natural progression.  Before the big wheels the baby should be erect in a walker, and pushed around.  All this helps strengthens the baby's muscles.

### SKILL 8.2  Cognitive Development of Infants

By two children can see if you are a boy or a girl.  This is determined by clothing and hairstyle.  By 6 or 7 children see gender as  more permanent.  They realize some characteristics are permanent.  Early on the girls separate from the boys on the playground.  Girls jump rope and the boys play  football.  In either group, the children want to be alike.  They use behaviors acceptable in their group only.

### SKILL 8.3  Social and Emotional Development of Infants

Social development is based on the role of reward and punishment in development.  This is not the only way to learn proper behavior.  Role modeling older people that know that girls wear dresses.  Women enter the door  first before the male.  Social interaction helps expose the children to the proper ways.  Boys learn early that society grants them more privileges than females.  Although the experiences a person is exposed  to and the situation will dictate the way either that man or woman will react.  There are other beliefs on gender development in the scientific community.  Some feel there are no biological ,social, or emotional differences in male or female babies.  This difference in development after birth because of the individuals exposure to various role models.  This is all a learned response.  So that gender role behaviors are deeply woven into our culture.

## SKILL 8.4 Infant care: feeding, bathing, dressing, and disciplining

For the infant there are bottles or breast feeding every three-four hours including in the middle of the night. You don't start solid foods like baby cereal until four to six months. This extra feeding should help the little one sleep through he night. Once the umbylical cord falls off the baby can have a lukewarm bath. I know my oldest son was less than five pounds and healthy, yet squirmy. I laid a towel on the kitchen counter and had ready the no-tear baby shampoo, soap, washcloth, lotion powder, and a hooded infants towel. I put the warm water in my largest mixing bowl right in a clear kitchen sink. I dipped my son in the water. I lathered his washcloth with neutrogena soap, a gentle product. Never let go of the baby. Lather the body. Dip in bowl of water. Last lather shampoo on those few hairs. Then rinse out the no tear baby shampoo. Next powder all the cracks. Put on Desitin for the baby rash on the genitals. Try on a diaper. Be sure to see the pediatrition monthly. Dress the baby in comfortable loose buttons or designs that the baby could tear off and choke on. As far as disciplining an infant it shouldn't be done. Never hold up a baby and shake it. This can actually kill the infant. Don't put in a room alone very long. When a baby complains and fusses there is a problem. Be loving and patient enough to figure out what this bundle of joy means. Then take care of it.

## SKILL 8.5 Physical and Motor Development of Toddlers

Each child has a style of growth which is unique to him and no one else. As a toddler he can hold his head up. The arms and hands are still controlled by the head and eyes. The baby can reach for things. The baby is now able to extend his feet and legs and support his weight. At twelve weeks or three months the baby can stand alone. At two and a half months he will sit alone. But the baby will walk alone at one year old. The baby can pickup and put most anything in the mouth. At one the baby can pull up on the couch.

## SKILL 8.6 Cognitive Development of Toddlers

At this point the baby is going to an upright position as a toddler. At one year the baby can form a three word sentence. Now more than ever the language will begin to develop at two years old. Teeth will come in between one and four. The child grows two inches and three pounds. Sleeping all night of course, plus a two hour afternoon nap. At two the baby is motor minded. He is active. Even his small motor skills are developing like sticking out the tongue. The two year old can hold a cup of milk in one hand. The more exposure to many things will awaken your baby to the magnificence world around.

## SKILL 8.7 Social and Emotional Development of Toddlers

At two the child is still self-centered. He parallel plays when with other children his age. This means they are beside each other in a sandbox. They work on their own project, never together this young. Emotionally he is developing. He can laugh with family and friends. He shows pity, sympathy, and shame. He may even pout. He can show guilt when doing something wrong. As of three years old the word use increases. The agility is seen when the child runs. The three year old enjoys order and tidiness. Many more questions are asked as the child becomes more perceptive. Don't forget words at three is good normal development. Now the parent can start to bargain with the three year old. Jealousy is possible in a three year old. He needs no help with eating at three either.

## SKILL 8.8 Toddler Care: Feeding, Bathing, Dressing, Disciplining, and Safety

Most toddlers need 3000 calories per day. If The food is not provided many parts of the body would suffer. Malnutrition causes many problems like a lag, in height. The child will lack energy too. The child needs to follow the Food Guide Pyramid. A toddler loves foods that he can pick up with his fingers. That's bananas, muffins, and fruit for breakfast. Lunch can be small cut up sandwiches and fruit with chocolate milk. You still need to encourage eating and assisting the toddler. Pretty much a toddler can feed themselves. Dinner could be cut up meat and vegetables. Bathing can be easier with the toddler than the infant. Fill the tub with 2-4 inches of lukewarm water. You can purchase a plastic seat with suctions on the bottom that hook to the tub for safety. Use a mild no tear baby shampoo. Use a washcloth. Put floating toys in the tub. Have a dry towel close by. Toddlers like to dress themselves. They may put it on backwards, but let them. Be sure to praise the child's efforts. As a toddler, disciplining could be time out. If a toddler gets out of hand and all wound up and is past the point of listening, remove him too a safe timeous spot, like his bedroom or a certain chair. Don't put him anywhere he can get into trouble. But when hitting someone, grabbing things, yelling at someone , or simply refusing to do what is asked can send the child to time out. During timeout the child should realize his wrong behavior. A toddler can get all around the house. Be sure the cupboards, cabinets, and drawers have safety latches put on so the child cannot open these area. Put poisonous cleaners in a high locked cabinet. Lock the basement door. Unplug and tie up cords on unused electrical appliances. Cover the unused electrical outlets. Toddlers can put something like a penny and get electrocuted. Soon the toddler is ready to start toilet training..

## SKILL 8.9  Preschool Physical and Motor Development

There are five major development areas.  The muscles grow, the nervous system grows, and so does the glands.  The child's physical condition includes normal blood sugar, water balance, oxygen use, and more.  Growth comes in periods or phases.  At this time  the child may grow a quick two inches.  Then the next growth spurt won't be until puberty.  During these growth spurts the child required more nourishment.

Motor development is when the baby gets control over the body's muscles.  During the first year of life the infant struggles to get control of its own body.  This process actually begins during the fifth month of pregnancy, when the mom begins to feel movement.  The child works to gain control over gross movements - like walking, swimming, and running up until five years old.  By six the child is ready.  Most motor development has at least been started.  Now to be perfected.  Those toddlers that exercise have better mental health.  Motor control allows the young child to entertain themselves.  The child can socialize.  And last the child can reach independence.  Motor development relates to the child's self-concept.  Not only does the child's motor development affect his self-concept and personality; but his personality affects his motor development.  It's a circular reaction.

Development of muscle control depends on the child's maturity.  Learning cannot occur until the body is matured and developed.  There are different rates of this motor development.  It starts with the head, the trunk, the arms, the hands, the legs, and the feet.  During stage one, the eye coordination and smile develop.  The second stage is to develop the trunk.  That is working to sit up alone.  The third stage is for reaching and grasping.  Now to develop the legs and feet.  First is rolling, then crawling.  Finally pulling up to a standing position.  By one you'll see signs of walking.  Once upright life takes on a whole new viewpoint.

## SKILL 8.10  Cognitive Growth

At the second birthday a child starts to know what is proper and acceptable and what is not.  As age increased the child got better at solving a problem.  Memory     improves greatly  around two.  During the first  two years of life the child  merely plays  with the small toys.  He'll toss and chase the ball.  During the last part of year two a child starts to group toys.  At two many children like imitating.  If an adult shows the child a certain way to play with the toys sure enough the child will repeat the same act with the toys over and over,  The infant starts to imitate adult behavior by ten months.  Acts of aggression appear in younger children than two year olds.  By two this child should know about nine words.

## SKILL 8.11  Social and Emotional Development of Preschoolers

Rewards help motivate a preschooler to do the right thing. If a preschooler matures and has a successful social adjustment, they'll have a good self-concept. If there's a poor adult role model in the home, it can harm the preschooler. There are four things too check if a person is well adjusted socially. First group acceptance. Second any group acceptance. Third is their attitude toward the others in the group. Last is how much pleasure the one gets from the group.

Conformity is forced on society by human pressure, peer pressure. Society only accepts a little nonconformity. Children need friendships. This need for friends will increase as the child ages. The child will choose friends like him, same sex, same, age, and a good sport. Some young children invent imaginary friends. This is if they are lonely. There is nothing documented about imaginary friends being any problem. Getting a 3-4 year old a pet is terrific. If the child can feed and give water to the pet, they are learning to care for another. This is a skill necessary for a future relationship and family. Preschoolers shift friends often. One day at the nursery school two play together. The next day they both play with other friends, but there's no hard feelings between the two. Friends fill the need for companionship and help the young person continue socialization. Group or gangs can be a bad influence on a teen. Popularity judges social acceptance. More friends means more popular. Respect and acceptance is fulfilled in a group of friends Children that are friendly and cooperative tend to rate higher in a group of friends. The following factors can lead to social acceptance. Makes a good first impression. Looks must be similar in style of clothes as the rest of the new group. Be in good physical condition. Brighter children put in better. They complete their schoolwork without any trouble. If your near the group and you begin new friendships, you will be part of the group soon enough. The child from a happy home will fit into the group easier. Children bond better with other children from the same socioeconomic status. It is important for social acceptance that the child develops skills to be self-confident, creative, and original. Be creative, and outgoing. Unfortunately popularity is judged by many parents, teachers, and peers as an indication of the child's success in social adjustments.

Emotions are present when a baby is born. Emotions are not learned. A baby can express happiness and displeasure at being moved. Even by one year the older adult can recognize how an infant feels. Is it anger, joy, fear, happiness, or hate on the baby's face? Emotions are part of heredity. Yet the environment has its part too. Development of the glands-effect emotional behavior. Temperament is like mood, but it is permanent. It is a mix again of heredity and environment. Children must have both pleasant and sad emotional experiences to be able to reach the perfect medium. Emotions are influenced by learning and must be controlled. Children's emotions are short lived. These emotions are intense. Children's emotions are transitory, having quick shifts. These emotions are frequent and very different. Emotions can be detected by behavior. They can change in strength. How the emotions are expressed can be changed.

Common childhood patterns of emotions would be seen with fear, worry,anxiety,anger,jealousy,curiosity,joy,pleasure,delight,and affection. The people in the baby's life will help them control these emotions. Control can be learned by imitation of how to handle the emotion. Direct teaching of how to respond to an emotion properly is helpful too. All emotional states are prepared for physically and glandulary. Many a child will respond to an emotion with moodiness, regression, and explosions. Here's some idea on emotions. There is no best way to express an emotion. If you always react one way to an emotion. It is hard to change that routine. It is good to talk over what's bothering you with a friend. Exercise helps relieve pent up emotions.

### SKILL 8.12 Preschooler care, feeding, bathing, dressing, disciplining, and safety.

Feeding is easy. A preschooler needs the foods on the Food Guide Pyramid. That's fruits, vegetables, dairy products, grains, also some meats. Plenty of water is important. Finger foods are a good choice. Have french toast strips and juice for breakfast. Try a sandwich cut into fours with carrot and celery sticks for lunch. Dinner is a small portion of a protein with a vegetable and a salad. Drink milk and you are all set. Bathing alone is okay, if you supervise. Never leave a small child alone in the bathtub. The child can use a washcloth. He can use a towel to dry off. He can brush his teeth with a little help. It's easier for a preschooler to remove clothes than put them on. This involves learned motor skills. By five a child can completely dress themselves. Tying shoelaces doesn't develop until 6 years old. That's why velcro tennis shoes are better until the child can tie shoelaces. Buttons, zippers, and buckles are a problem at first. Discipline is a training process for growth and development. It is used to mold the child to the ways of their culture. So that discipline is like education and counseling to gain self-control. It helps pre-schools learn the limits. This way they too will act appropriately. Without rules, a child would do as he pleases. The discipline must be consistent or the child is lost. Positive motivation in the form of reward helps children conform. There are many kinds of punishment. It should be given immediately after wrong doing. All children learn better under a gentle hand, and an encouraging smile. But don't use rewards too often. There's three disciplinary categories. They are authoritarian with strict rules. That's control through force. There's democratic techniques where the parents use reason to explain a desired behavior of a child. Education rather than punishment. There's allot of praise in the democratic method. Permissive is the third disciplinary technique. That's when there is little or no discipline. There's no family guidance on how to act. There's no punishment. This leaves behavior decisions up to the children. It's not fair to these children either. Good discipline must be firm, fair, and consistent. Authoritarian discipline leaves its mark on the children. This is the strictest form of disciplining. An over disciplined child sees society as mean and hostile. If a child is raised on punishment and rejection, it will turn to fear. Permissive discipline simply confuses a child. They become fearful and aggressive. Democratic discipline promotes social adjustments.

Safety is important for a preschooler. Leave the child locks on the drawers and cabinets. Keep the electrical outlets that are not being used covered. Be sure any toxic chemical are locked in a high, hard to reach area. If little pieces come with a toy careful. The child may want to put those pieces into their mouth. He could choke. Remove the tiny pieces before someone chokes. Your child's safety should be in the front of your mind at all times.

## SKILL 8.13 Physical and Motor Development of School-age Children

The child physical development determines his abilities. What games he'll be good at. We break down physical development into four areas. First is the nervous system that develops. Second is muscle growth. Now the child enters the games and sports. Third is the development of the glands Fourth is all the systems inside working correctly, like blood, use of oxygen, and water balance. Rapid growth from birth until two years old. Puberty is the next large growth spurt. Then just after puberty another growth spurt at sixteen years old.

## SKILL 8.14 Cognitive Development of Schooling Children

Social cognition as a form of questioning or investigation. It's a body of knowledge. This goes along with Piglets mental development theories. Children's social knowledge is not figured out on their own. It is taught via discipline or in a group of children.

## SKILL 8.15 Social and Emotional Development of School-age Children

Social development is acting in an acceptable manner among my peers. To be socialized takes three steps. First is when children behave like their peers. The second part is doing right in the group's social roles. Third the children must be social, like other people. Most want to conform to the way the group performs. They want to know what is right or wrong. The family helps you make good relationships. Social interaction techniques should be learned early. Exposure to social activities early is necessary too. The pattern of physical and emotional development is similar in all children. At birth the baby doesn't care for others around. During the third month the baby will cry until held or talked to. By the sixth month the baby is smiling. By a year old the child can walk and begin to talk. In early childhood if attending a preschool children make social friends. This is a great way to develop. Before two children parallel play. That's stand beside each other but play separately. In elementary school, the children want many friends and that's many friends at one time. At puberty children drop the gang of friends and prefer to be alone. Reversals in attitudes and behaviors will take place. Adolescents often don't like the changes in their body so they act different towards everyone else. Actually they became antisocial. If the teen remains antisocial, it can be harmful to the future relationships he has. For emotional development to be healthy the child has no emotional deprivation. The child experiences all kinds of emotional experiences. Parents that never pick up the infant deprive him of affection. That lack of affection is neglect. It's a form of rejection. Babies deprived of affection do not thrive.

They develop slower physically. Motor development slows down . Speech is delayed. Intellectual development is even damaged. These children find it hard to get along with others. Emotional deprivation increases the chance of a maladjusted personality.

Intellectual development results when the child perceive new stimuli. The endocrine system or glands respond to stimuli. Learning starts in one of three ways. One is by trial and error. Then imitation. Last by conditioning when you see it over and over. As you mature you develop your emotions and you learn better control. Children's emotions are intense, frequent, shifting, individualized, change in strength, and show up in the same symptoms. These are some common emotions for school age children. embarrassment, worry, anxiety, anger, jealousy, grief, curiosity ,joy, and affection. It's important to maintain emotional control. If getting out of hand try exercise, look at the funny side, talk to a friend, or listen to music.

### SKILL 8.16  School-aged childcare: feeding, bathing, dressing, disciplining, and safety

Children of school-age still need to eat by the Food Guide Pyramid. They need six to eleven grains, three-five fruits, four to six vegetables, two dairy products, and two meats, three ounces only. Add six to eight glasses of water. Use very little salt, sugar, and oils. This is about 3000 calories a day. These children are old enough to take a bath or shower on their own. Use shampoo every few days. These children dress themselves. Adolescents try to dress differently to rebel against society. For disciplining, feel tough love will keep your teen out of trouble. Under no means go soft on a misbehaving child. Remember adults are the role models. You are the boss. Again discipline is education to gain self-control. Rules must be followed. Discipline must be firm-fair-and-consistent. Positive rewards work better than punishment. Punishment sets up resentment. Education not punishment is necessary. Safety is having any broken electrical wire or glass fragments picked up right away. Don't leave out toys to trip over. Falls send many people to the hospital. If water spills wipe it up. Water and electricity don't mix. If you touch it you'll get a shock.

## SKILL 8.17 Physical, emotional, social, and intellectual development of the adolescent.

Puberty is the time of adolescence. It is the end of childhood. The physical beginning of adulthood. The physical changes come about in a four year period. The sex organs become useful. Girls start menstruation around thirteen. The pituitary gland and the gonads initiate the physical changes. The growth hormone sets up body size. The hypothalamus gland starts all the changes in puberty. At this time the child may grow four too six inches and put on ten to twenty pounds. This is when boys get hair on their face and body. Girls get breasts. Boys voices get deeper. The muscles develop and are stronger. Most adolescence find it hard to adjust to their physical changes. They usually vent with negative emotions like moodiness, irritability, and unhappiness. Many interests change now. Adolescence is a hectic time emotionally. Most these teens are not thrilled with the body changes. This promotes unhappiness and deviant behavior. In adolescence people grow away from their parents. They form close relationships with their peers. Peers form tight knit groups similar to gangs. They become independent from adults. They learn group loyalty and standards. They learn responsibilities for the group. Here the children help each other reach independence. They feel the emotional satisfaction from friendships. They no longer feel insecure. Over sensitiveness stems from a desire to be accepted by the peer group. Competition is part of gang life. That is competition between group members, between other groups and your group , or with adults. Responsibilities in the group are vital.

Socially at puberty group activities are replaced with solitude. With the quick growth of the brain during puberty came the increase of mental abilities. Reasoning increases. The child can make better personal and social adjustments.

## SKILL 8.18 Relationships for Adolescents; dating , friends, and family

Adolescence marks the development sexually of boys and girls. The glands start off the increase in size and functioning of the sexual parts. Now opposites attract. Dating is started. More couples or groups of couples are going out and less gang activities are taking place. Friends are very important. Fitting in still is a top priority. Family is loosing it's importance. Friends fill your need for love and attention. Parents are left far behind. Dating is almost an experiment to see what type you would want to marry in the future.

**COMPETENCY 9.0  NUTRITION**                                    **3.1%**

**SKILL 9.1  Diet and Health**
The Dietary Guidelines for Americans set up by the government is six simple rules for eating healthy.  Eat a variety of foods.  Maintain your ideal weight according to the height/weight chart at yoour local doctor.  Avoid fat and cholesterol.  Eat enough starch and fiber.  Avoid too much sugar.  Avoid too much salt..  If you follow these simple six rules you'll be eating better.  If you're eating better you will be in optimal working condition.  Eat right and exercise for better health.  Wellness is health of the entire person.  Health of the entire person.  Health physically,mentally, and emotionally.  If one of these three are off kilter,that can effect the other two.  Wellness is when all three are in order.  Take care of your own health.  The body does alot and needs proper fuel from food.  The body has to digest food, circulate the blood, which carries O2 and nutrients throughout the body.  There's a constant cell replacement.  There's the waste-disposal system that gets rid of waste from the body.

If you are overweight eat a variety of foods.  Spice up your food.  Eat low calorie foods.  Eat plenty of vegetables.  Six little meals are better for your metabolism than three meals.  Drink eight glasses of water.  One before each meal or snack.  Eat your meal on a smaller salad plate.  Eat slowly.  Becareful at a party.  Keep track of your weight losses.  Weigh every five to seven days.

**SKILL 9.2  Nutritional Information, like RDA**
RDA stands for Recommended Daily Allowance.  The Food and Nutrition Board of the National Academy of Sciences.  They study nutrient needs.  The RDA Chart shows by age group, height, and weight what amount of which nutrient is needed.  If you're an athlete or pregnant you'll need more nutrients.  Good nutrition is when you eat the right amount.  Poor nutrition can cause over weight, illness, and tooth decay.  People with poor nutrition develop, malnutrition.  It could be a deficiency, a one nutrient severe shortage.  Sometimes an over weight person is eating only junk, ends up malnurished.  Skipping necessary nutrients will cause problems for the body.  The following nutrients must list the RDA amount in various products.

Protein, vitamin A,C,D,B6, thiamine, riboflavin, niacin, calcium, iron, folic acid, and phosphorus are all in a serving of cereal.  You need all these nutrients.  Read the RDA on the food label.  If that's too confusing take a one a day multiple vitamin.

The nutritional label has just as much information.  Read it.  It tells serving size, servings per container, calories per serving, grams of protein, carbohydrates, and fats per serving.  It may or may not list the cholesterol per serving.  Amount of sodium will be listed.  Check the dates on the foods ecspecially if the food will spoil.  Open dating has four kinds.  The Pack date tells when the product was manufactured and packaged.  There's the pull date or sell date when it should be removed from the stores shelves.  There's the

25                                              **HOME ECONOMICS**

freshness date which means the product will be best before the date printed. There's the expiration date when you should throw out the product.

### SKILL 9.3 Six Major Nutrients and Their Functions

Carbohydrates are simple and complex. They help the body use proteins to make every body cell. Carbohydrates should be 55% of your daily food intake. Fats are necessary every day to transport specific vitamins throughout the body. Proteins are 75% of all the solid matter in the body and part of every cell. Antibodies to fight diseases come from proteins. Vitamins are substances found in food that helps a body function. Vitamin C fights infections. It's in oranges.

There are about 17 common vitamins taken in food daily or take it in pill form. Minerals found in food is needed for the body to work efficiently. Minerals become a part of the body like calcium becomes strong teeth and bones. The minerals are part of the body like iron for blood. There are two major mineral groups. The first occurs in large amounts in the body and food. They are calcium, phosphorus, magnesium, chlorine, potassium, and sodium. Calcium and phosphorus work closely in nutrient teamwork to make healthy strong bones and teeth. Osteopororsis is a brittle bone disease of the elderly if they didn't get enough calcium as a child. Magnesium is a mineral that helps the nervous system. It's found in green leafy vegetables. Iron helps the blood by carrying oxygen through the body. Liver is a good source of iron. If people lack iron, they may be anemic. Iodine from salt helps the thyroid gland work correctly. Zinc helps the body use proteins, fats, and carbohydrates.

The sixth important nutrient is water. The body is majority water. Thus it must be cleansd daily. You should drink 6-8 glasses of water daily. The water cools the body temperature. The water is the main part of the blood. The water helps the removal of body wastes.

### SKILL 9.4 Nutrient Food Sources

Fat-soluble vitamins likeA,D,E,+K come from yellow fruits and vegetables like carrots and spinach or milk. Some of the cooking oils have fat-soluble vitamins in it. Water-soluble vitamins like B1, B2 ,B3, B6, B12, and vit. C are in pork, bread, and cereal, cheese, eggs, poultry, nuts, and citrus fruits. Minerals are in liver, milk, pinach, salt, meats, and eggs. Carbohydrates are in bread and cereals and sugars. Proteins in all meats, nuts, and legumes. Of course, water is in water. It's a must to cleanse your system.

### SKILL 9.5 Nutritional Needs by Age, Sex, and Stress

Everyone needs the same basic nutrients. Simply look at the food pyramid. You need 6-11 carbohydrates, the staff of life, bread, cereal,rice,pasta, and grains. All people need 3-5 vegetable servings daily. You need 2-4 fruits. Have 2-3 servings of milk, yogurt, and cheese. Use fats and oils,sugars, and salts sparingly. You eat these foods to be healthy. The nutrients in the food helps the body build and repair cells,keep vital body processes working, and create energy. The human body needs six kinds of nutrients: proteins, carbohydrates, fats, vitamins, minerals, and water. These nutrients work together as teams in your body. Your body can use only a certain amount of each nutrient.

As you mature or change your lifestyle,your nutrient needs change. Scientific research is continuing to discover new facts about nutrients. The Food and Nutrition Board of the National Academy of Sciences-National Research Council develops the Food Guide Pyramid along with the RDA(Recommended Dietary Allowances). The RDA chart specifies:age groups,weights,and heights and what nutrients are needed by which age groups. For instance a teenager is more active than his mom. He needs more food for energy. A pregnant woman needs more nutrients because she's feeding two. There are about 50 different nutrients nutrients discovered already. Males can eat more than woman. Women need about 2400 calories a day. Men need 3600 calories a day because their metabolisms work faster than ladies.

When it comes to stress,you actually need extra calories or more foods. Stress wears down your body, to build it up fill it with great nutrients.

### COMPETENCY 9.6 Diets for Infants, Young Children, Middle-aged, Elderly, a Pregnant Woman, and Individuals With Special Health Problems.

Infant diets should include liquid programs like Similac. Of course, breast feeding is the most ideal food for a newborn. The breastfeeding helps mom and baby bond. The breastmilk has natural antibodies and nutrients to keep the baby healthy. The advantage in bottle feeding is that other family members can assist in feeding the little one. Att four to six months the baby can eat solid foods. Begining solid foods are cereal, vegetables, fruits, meats, poultry, and fish. All these foods are cooked, mashed, and strained. That's the convenience of Gerber or any bought baby food. Mix the different food groups. Babies should never be greasy or spicy foods.

Children need varying nutrients. They need small portions. They need two-three servings of milk if under nine years old. Nine to twelve, you should need three or more dairy products. Young children need one serving from vitamin A, C, and two,or more fruits and vegetables every day. Two servings of meat daily. Four servinhs of bread or cereal will finish off the young child's daily diet. Teens and teen athletes need more food and nutrients with a lot of water.

Middle aged adults are fully grown. They lead sedentary lives and less food is needed. Twenty per cent of the United States households have someone living there alone. They arre in danger of poor eating habits. Poor eating habits can end up in fatigue,depression,lack of energy, and frequent colds.

The elderly that's one out of ten people die over sixty-five. Some have special eating diets. They still need the same nutrients they did as a child. The metabolism is slowing down. Thus the elderly need fewer calories. They need a varied diet, high in nutrients but low in calories. Some elderly have the biggest meal of the day at noon. Having six small meals is better than three large meals. Long lasting and recurring conditions make it hard for the elderly to eat right. Maybe dental problems, or high cholesterol, is the reason for not wanting to eat. Transportation to shop and then cook may be too much. Some don't care to eat out of loneliness. If necessary try to get meal on wheels. They deliver already prepared meals that need only to be heated.

Remember a pregnant woman is eating for two. She must get extra calories about 1250 a day. She needs 65% more protein with more fruits and vegetables too. This will give more nutrients to both mom and baby.

If you're recovering from a serious illness or surgery, you may need a special diet. First would be a clear liquid diet. This is low in protein, vitamin, minerals, fiber, and calories. Drinks allowed are coffee, tea, soft drinks, fruit drinks, and gelatin. A soft diet is easy-to-digest-foods with no fiber, no raw fruits, or vegetables.

Other health problems like diabetes, ulcers, high blood pressure, and heart trouble usually have special diets. A vegetarian diet is based on plant foods. Foods eaten vegetables, fruits, breads, cereals, nuts, and seeds are on the vegetarian diet. There's the macrobiotic diet which is mainly brown rice for all meals. There are low salt diets, low-cholesterol diets, certain allergies, are bothered by specia foods.

## SKILL 9.7 Nutrients Deficient in the U.S. Population

Deficiencies are a problem because they are a severe shortage of one or more nutrients. An example would be lack of iron causes a blood anemia. A lack of fat or carbohydrates, force your body to use proteins for energy. If you feel tired and lack vitality. Their diets lack fiber, thus constipation.

Vitamin A from liver, yellow vegetables, and spinach, If you get too little your eyes get oversensitive to light. You might get nightblindness. Your resistance to infections is lowered. Vit. D. from sunlight and milk. If too little vitamin D the bones and teeeth get soft and weak. Phosphorus stays in the kidneys. It could lead to kidney stones. Vitamin E from oils and bread and cereal if low will cause the blood cells may rupture. Vitamin K is in green leafy vegetables and potatoes. It helps blood clot. If lacking,infants may hemorrhage. They'll get jaundice. Vitamin B1 is in pork, liver, breads, and cereals. If you don't have enough vitamin B1,you could have mental confusion,swelling of the heart, leg cramps,and skin diseases. Vitamin B2 from milk and eggs,breads, and cereals.

If lacking your lips crack. Niacin found in fish, poultry, bread, and cereals. If lacking skin cracks and there is mental anxiety. Vitamin B6 is from meats, cereals, and breads.If not enough you get dry, cracked lips, anemia, and depression. Vitamin B12 from liver, eggs, and meats.

If it's lacking anemia, fatigue,and loss of balance will set in. Pantothenic acid is in eggs, breads, and cereals. Without it you get fatigue and stomach cramps. Biotin is from liver,peanuts, and dark green vegetables. Lack of Biotin causes vomiting, depression, and loss of appetite. Folic acid from eggs, dark green leafy vegetables, and wheat germ, when lacking, causes anemia. Vitamin C is in citrus fruits. If lacking gums bleed, weight loss, get sick easier, and weakness. If the diet lacks iodine,a goiter could develop. If you lack zinc you'll have a poor appetite. Some food deficiencies are due to lack of knowledge of needed foods for the body. Other reasons could be like lack of money, lack of cooking skills, and loneliness. If an elderly person can't wear their dentures, try baby food that is pureed. Watch sodium levels and cholesterol. Keep them low. Some people have some food allergies causing symptoms of illness too. A lack of calcium and phosphorus result in deformed bones or rickets. You need calcium for blood clotting. Potassium,sodium, and chlorine are rarely lacking.

## SKILL 9.8  Nutrient Deficiencies and Overdoses

| Nutrient | Deficiencies | Overdoses |
|---|---|---|
| Vitamin A | Night blindness/cracked skin | headaches/nausea |
| Vitamin D | Deformed Bones | diarrhea/kidney stones |
| Vitamin E | | Weakened Muscles |
| Nausea/dizziness/fatigue | | |
| Vitamin K | Bleeding in Babies/Weak bones | jaundice in children |
| Vitamin B1(Thiamin) | Mental Confusion/heart swells/leg cramps | unknown |
| Vitamin B2(riboflavin) | cracked lips/sore tongue/skin disorders | unknown |
| Niacin | sore mouth/cracked skin/anxiety | ulcers/higher sugar level |
| Vitamin B6 | skin disorders/nausea/anemia | joint stiffness |
| Vitamin B12 | fatigue/depression loss of balance | unknown |
| Pantothenic Acid | stomach cramps/vomiting fatigue/can't sleep | need more thiamin |
| Biotin | vomiting/fatigue/depression | unknown |
| Folic Acid | bleeding gums/weakness | diarrhea/kidney stones |
| Vitamin C | scurvy/lack of appetite | diarrhea |
| Calcium | Osteopororsis | unknown |

## SKILL 9.9 Nutrient Toxicities

When some fat soluble vitamins buildup in the blood it can be toxic. First symptoms would be a headache. Then the rest of the week you will feel like you have the flu. You have a temperature. You get nausea, diarrhea, weight loss, and weakness due to the overdose of vitimins A, D, E, or K.

## COMPETENCY 10.0  KNOWLEDGE OF PARENTING                    3.1%

### SKILL 10.1  Parenting styles on Growth and Development

There are three styles of parenting.  The strictest form is called authoritarian.  This still has set rules with punishment if the rules aren't followed.  Control is by force.  Dominated children can develop inferiority complexes.  Being told what to do all of the time causes the child to mistrust his own judgment.  The democratic technique lies in the middle.  Here the parents use reason to explain the desired behavior.  Education not punishment is the style.  Use a lot of praise for right doing.  Permissive is the third style of parenting.  Here anything goes.  No discipline is used .  The family doesn't guide behavior at all.  There's no punishment.

Growth and development for any child will blossom if the democratic style of parenting is used.  The child will develop right on time, according to all the growth charts.  The authoritarian family may stunt growth and development of the child.  The permissive style of parenting opens the child up to raising himself near kinds of deviant behavior.

### SKILL10.2  Methods of Child Guidance and Discipline

Discipline means for the child to follow the family's rules.  It is doing the right thing at the right time.  If a child is never disciplined, he'll lack respect for all authority.  Even adolescence crave guidance from parents.  Even though they don't show it.  Baby boomers, that's parents now in their 40's and 50's.must set limits for their children.  Permissiveness is out.  Parents must exercise their rules at least up to sixteen.  Parents must go on with rules on smoking, drinking, and curfew right up to eighteen, college age.  Some high schools believe parents rules last until twenty one when college is over.  Discipline rests on love and child support.  Parents that resort to punishment and   threats should see what's wrong with their relationships with their children.  Again discipline must be firm-fair-consistent  as said by Dr. Lena Bailey of Ohio State University.  Any punishment should be given just after the bad deed.  It should be equal to the misdeed.  Some children  prefer physical punishment like a spanking because it's swift and over quickly.  Some children hate if the parents are angry with them.  Thus a spanking is over quickly.  Taking away a well liked toy for a punishment works.  Say no Sega games for one week.  Don't tell the child the punishment over and  over.  Administer the required punishment, like one hour in your room and clean it up.  Then give a period of time for the room to be cleaned.  If you plan to yell at the child, do this in private, never in front of friends.  Don't rebuke the child with angry tones.  He will shut you out.  Parents shouldn't curse when scolding any child.  The parents should suggest better ways to handle the problem that the child had.  This way he can correct it next time.  Both punishments and rewards mold the personalities of our children.  Rewards are valuable.  Don't use them as bribes.  They'll loose their meaning.

Time out is a good means of punishment for negative behavior.  Physical punishment like spanking with a hand or a belt is never the answer.  Some parents feel the child won't know who's the boss if you spare the rod and spoil the child. any corporal punishment is inappropriate. Beating and whipping will decrease a child's verbal development. Actually time out works the best. at least better than physical punishment.

Now on the other hand should good deeds be rewarded, like good grades, cleaning their bedroom, mowing the lawn, or taking out the trash? There are several methods of child guidance and discipline. Authoritarian is when the parents expect total obedience. If not punishment is the answer. Permissive is another stye of parenting. Here the children do as they please and always get their way. The children do not respect the parents during all this freedom. The middle type of discipline is called democratic. Here the parents set rules or limits. This makes it easier for a child to behave. Then if a rule or limit is broken the parent will explain the wrong doing. Then a punishment to fit the crime is awarded like folding the laundry, mop the floor, or mow the lawn. if old enough. So discipline helps one set limits for conduct or behavior. When giving punishments, don't yell. use a soft, cool, tone of voice. Make the discipline fit the misbehavior. Be sure to discipline immediately after the wrong doing. Children raised in an authoritarian household had trouble making decisions later in life because they were always told what to do. Children raised in democratic households were better motivated and higher achievers.

## SKILL 10. 3 Discipline or Guidance for Different Individuals

In olden times children dressed like adults, but were socially seen and not heard . Children were meant obey. Now though children no longer must look like mini adults. Since Piaget's findings where we see children are far different in development from adults. Strict means of punishment were still acceptable with early American settlers. Religions set up the first rules for society.

If you have an aggressive strong willed child, you may not work when you try time out. Then try taking away something the child likes, maybe a television show, or a Sega game for the entire week. This child may need a bit of controlled physical discipline. If you don't get the child too listen and cooperate while young, he'll run into all sorts of problems in the future when he doesn't get his way. If your child is shy and with an inferiority complex and disobeys, maybe time out with an explanation of how the bad act could hurt somebody else will be enough. Democratic families use the explanation mode mostly. If the family uses permissive discipline and the child never misbehaves, you are fortunate. But little if any direction is given to the child in the permissive family. Let's say the child calls the little girl next door names like freckle face or carrot top for the red head. The permissive parent says oh how cute. While the little girls parents are angry. They tell the boys parents to teach him that name calling is wrong. Right there the boy's parents are doing him a disservice. He'll have to pick up right from wrong later in life and not from his parents. At least he could have been made to apologize to the little girls. Names don't help anyone.

## SKILL 10.4   Children Services

First of all parents need to take the children to the doctor and the dentist yearly. If there's a problem like illness see the doctor right away. If for some reason the child is acting out with aggression or just the opposite. He won't say a word. He's introverted. Actually completely withdrawn. See a counselor, like a psychologist. Daycare if researched can be very useful. Not only with the child be learning how to interact socially. He'll be taken care of and mom can have some free time. Daycares need to be throughly checked over. Is it clean? Are there enough adults for the number of children. Is there a playgroung? What is the daily routine? Do you pay if absent? Of course, there's cost. There are other programs at the YMCA or JCC like Mommy and me or baby gymnastics. If you can get your child into extracurricular programs, Do. Preschoolers brains are like sponges, they soak up everything. Never will they be able to learn and retain at such a quick rate.

## SKILL 10.5  Learning Environment for Infants and the Young

Any safe home can be a learning environment for a young child. Certain television shows on Public Broadcasting teach morals with some of the specials. The first place the infant began learning was when the mom picked him upright. Those eyes began to scan the room. All types of new things. Anything new and exciting for the children will be a learning environment. That's why it's good to start kindergarten if not preschool to start learning as soon as possible.

## COMPETENCY 11.0 STRESS AND CRISIS

### SKILL 11.1 Family Crisis

A crisis is an event for which old ways to handle it are no longer helpful. Most families are effected by a crisis at least once in your life. Crisis are things like divorce, widowhood, alcoholism, extramarital affairs, having a baby, unemployment, imprisonment, or spouse abuse.

### SKILL 11.2 Impacts of Various Crisis

There's always a consequence after a crisis. Divorce will separate one of the parents from the children daily. Sure there will be holiday and summer get together. But not seeing your parent daily, you loose allot of the teachings that parents have for the children. Widowhood's similar to loosing the daily contact with the absent parent only you never see the deceased parent. The children may need counseling for the losses. Alcoholism effects the entire family. The parent drinking needs AA meetings and the family needs Alanon. Alcoholism may be a disease, but it's controllable. Cheating on your spouse is a crime. This can lead to divorce. Or the one cheating can see what he's loosing and messing up. He'll need counseling, possible with the rest of the family. What was his family lacking that forced him to look for love somewhere. Wise. Having a baby for the first time can be very exciting and scarry. The new little one will change the family forever. Concentrate on making the new part of the family welcome. Get the nursery ready together. Unemployment is a frightening position. Apply for unemployment benefits immediately. Start job hunting too. The rest of the family must make do and chip in if possible. Spouse abuse is unacceptable. Get away even if you have nothing. Get to a safe house. No one deserves to be abused. The abusive person needs help. Report the actions to the police.

### SKILL 11.3 Substance Abuse

If a family is not getting along and there's allot of yelling, they are in crisis. Out of this situation comes substance abuse. First pot, then hard narcotics. Now where's the money going? Straight to drugs. Maybe one spouse will pressure the other ,mate to join in and take the drugs. Everyone suffers. The children won't be cared for. The parents are destroying themselves. They haven't faced whatever the original problem was. Nothing gets solved.

### SKILL 11.4 Impacts from Substance Abuse

As I was saying earlier. Drug abuse or alcoholism will destroy life. They are expensive and deadly habits. Families split up. The abuser goes to a rehabilitation facility or jail if he steals to support his drug habit. Substance abuse is a black shadow over a family that could have been. No one will be friends with this family. People will see there's a problem.

### SKILL 11.5 Long-term illness stresses the family

If one of the family members has a long-term illness like Parkinsons Disease or Cancer, it would be difficult to care for them on a daily basis. But this caring for the ill can make the family closer. Those that resent taking their turn helping the ill one will be angry with their parents. Festered anger often explodes. Actually you should talk to your parents. Maybe there is another way you could be helpful, like doing the grocery shopping.. The family will have heightened emotions with the sick in the house. Find ways to relieve your stress. If it's exercise, listening to music, or talking to a friend. Money may be a problem with caring for a sick family member. Contact agencies that might help.

### SKILL 11.6 Breast and tentacular self-examination

These procedures should be performed once a month. Women stand in the show, press all around your breast.. You are looking for a lump that doesn't belong there. You will fell fatty deposits, but they are squishy, not, hard. You will feel your ribs. That's normal. For males after puberty you should check your male genitals. You are looking for unusual lumps or bumps. This is important so that you know what normal is. Look at the testes and penis. Then in the future if something seems abnormal, see a doctor.

### SKILL 11.7 Divorce and Family Structures Changes

First partners start to ignore each other. Then they stop being together. Next the ring is removed. Now the spouse moves out. But the divorce is not final until the judge declares the marriage is over. For some divorce is the most devastating emotional experiences. For others it is a stress reliever once they are out of the marriage. There's a big problem getting the father to pay child support. Children feel mixed results. They know they will be bounced between two parents.

### SKILL 11.8  Teen Pregnancy

Teen pregnancy is associated with dropping out of high school, poverty and low birth weight.  Over one million American teens get pregnant every year. Only half  have the babies. Many choose abortion or adoption.  Most of these teen pregnancies are not planned.  The United States is way over those born in France, England, or Canada.  But the baby born by a teenager could be premature.  If the teen doesn't  take care of herself the baby could be stillborn, born dead.  Teens if pregnant get to the clinic to get on a proper food program with vitamins.

### SKILL 11.9  Teen Pregnancy and Family Stressors

First of all the two future sets of grandparents and the new to be parents must meet.  Neither teen needs to drop cut of school if the older parents can help. Maybe one grandma will watch  the baby  three days and the other grandma will watch the other three days.  That leaves the happy teens to watch or take  the baby out on Sundays.  Both families will help with the cost of baby things.  The teen boy will get a job and pay as much as he can.  The teen mom will attend to that little one's laundry.  As long as the teens have help from their parents and they act responsible, it will work out fine.  The teens will have to give up their friends and extracurricular activities too.

### SKILL 11.10  Pregnant Teenager Alternatives

There are a number of alternatives for pregnant teenagers.  She may have her heart set on college, which doesn't include a baby.  This choice  would be an abortion.  Be sure to go to a reputable clinic and very early in the pregnancy. There's a beautiful idea of adoption.  You give up your child to an agency that picks parents that will spoil, love, and raise your child.  Remember you can raise your own  later when you are more settled and mature.  You can put you child in foster care.

### SKILL 11.11  Treatment for the abuser or one that neglects

Social workers can work with a family  to stop the physical abuse.  Sometimes at the house, the social worker is turned away.   If the family wants help, the social worker will visit  once a week.  She'll suggest ways to handle anger.  If the situation is bad, the social worker can get a court order to put the child in foster care.  The best treatment for the abusers is to be trained to react to children differently.  This is done at the hospital weekly where the sessions cover topics like, self- control, other ways to handle bad situations, and good childrearing procedures.  There are several videos shown where a mother practicality kills her daughter for spilling milk.  Then the same spilled milk situation handled with self-control.  At the sessions parents role play many rough situations and work them out gently.  The parents think of better ways to handle their own anger.

Call a friend, exercise, or try deep breathing. When parents always use physical punishment causes a  strained relationship because of the fear and mistrust. Using timeout and positive reinforcements raises a strong child.   Parents Anonymous at 1-800-421=0353 can help a parent  in trouble get control again in or the National Committee for the Prevention of Child Abuse can be contacted.

## SKILL 11. 12  Types of Child Abuse

Child abuse is any act between two and it's meant to harm someone.  It could be beating, burning, scalding, not feeding the child, or not taking a sick child  to the doctor.  Neglect  is when the parent doesn't  take responsibility and care for the child.  It's abused when the punishment is too harsh.

## SKILL 11.13  Causes of Child Abuse

There's many reasons for child abuse, but no excuses for it.  If a young teen feels trapped by an unwanted  pregnancy.  If the parents are unemployed, they may take it out on the children.  Parents prone too anger, alcohol, drugs, have low self-esteem, can't handle stress, has little self- control.  If a person was abused as a child, odds are these parents will continue the cycle and abuse their own children.

## SKILL 11.14  Symptoms of suicide

Suicide is highest among teenagers.  If an adolescent is going into a shell, no socializing.  There are few if any friends.  Alcohol or drugs could be messing up the teens thoughts.  Teenagers don't respect authority-like parents, teachers, or police.  They could feel very alone with  their problems.  Often teens are depressed.  Get these teens help quickly.  If they even mention suicide get a psychologist  to see  them right away.

## SKILL 11.15  How to Help the Depressed or Suicidal Individual

Take them to a psychologist.  She may need medication, like mood elevators.  Talk to the depressed.  Remind them of the good old days when life was fun.  Don't leave the person alone.  As long as she  has told you she wants to die, it is your duty to get help.  You could call Crisis Line  and get advice of what to do.

## SKILL 11.16  CPR cardiopulmonary resuscitation

Someone in every house should know CPR. Classes are offered at the Red Cross or American Heart Association. Most middle schools and high schools in Health class learn CPR. It's taught on a manikin named Annie. It's not a good idea to practice CPR on a real person, use pillow for practice. ABC is the starting call letters for CPR. A means open the airway. That's when you use the chin lift. B stands for breathing. Blow two quick full breaths into the victims mouth. Pinch the nose. C is for circulation. That's when you start compressions if there's no pulse. The ratio is 15-1. Remember if it's not broken, don't fix it. So when first arriving upon the injured, listen, and feel. This is checking for breathing. Do you feel their breath on your checks? If they're breathing check for pulse either on the neck or wrist. If no pulse get the compressions going. Send someone if possible to call 911. Keep your elbows straight. Push down about 1 ". Locate place for locked palms just below the sternum, middle of the rib cage. Don't stop doing the CPR until the victim recovers or help arrives. Even if you're exhausted, don't stop. You may save someone's life.

## SKILL11.17  Coping and eliminating stress

People cope with stress brought on by rapid change in a variety of ways. High blood pressure, getting an ulcer, or drinking all because of stress. Talking to someone, a friend or a psychologist is a healthy way to get rid of stress. There are several community agencies to help someone cope with stress. Call the public health department ,mental health centers, social service agencies. There are various self-help groups, like Parents Without Partners, widowed people, and Alcoholics Anonymous. Look in the yellow pages of the phone book for numbers for help. You need to cope with everyday stress without undue anxiety. People sense stress when lonely or not being wanted or needed. Everyone has some degree of stress. Good ways to cope are to take time to rest and play. Work on hobbies to relax. Exercise relieves tension and anger. try swimming, gardening, or walking. Grief is a form of stress when one close to you dies. It is painful. You need your loved ones and friends around for this. The loss of a parent is truely a lonely feeling. One is mentally healthy when the stresses of life are dealt out and you can cope easily. There are many symptoms of stress to recognize. Depression, anxiety, no interest in friends, family, or job. You can't concentrate or sleep. Confused about those around you. Headaches or hallucinations. Most mental problems can be diagnosed and treatable.

### SKILL 11.18 Family Crises

For each family crises there is a way to cope with it. When a baby is added to a family, the parents need to adjust to the situation. There's the cost as well as less sleep. If the couple set up a budget, this can be handled. A death like one of the grandparents, is rough on the family. Grief may require counseling. If there's illness, the family must pull together to help care for the ill one. With open communication you can be helpful source. But best of all during any problem the family must bond together. Divorce or separation is a big family problem. Therapy may be needed especially for the children to understand this change is not their fault.

### SKILL11.19 Support Systems

When individuals or families have problems who can they get support from? Well if the family can see it, they could get a therapist. The family must support the ailing one. Clergy of all faiths will help someone in need of assistance. Mental health centers in the yellow pages of the telephone book. Even the extended family can help. There are other public health assistance listed in the phone book. Schools have support for individuals through guidance counselors. They have a grief group, AA, and Anon. Yes the school can help too.

### SKILL 11.20 Agencies for Crisis Assistance

Many agencies have aid for those in need. There's the American Red Cross, YMCA, Government Social Services, food stamps, public housing, Al-Anon, Alateen, Alcoholics Anonymous, Mental health Centers, Administration for Aging, Hospice, Planned Parenthood, Health Clinics, Public Daycare, American Association of Retired People, American Automobile Association, American Cancer Society American Heart Association, CARE(Cooperative for American Relief Everywhere, Catholic Charities, Department of Health, Education, and Welfare, and the Food and Drug Administration.

**HOME ECONOMICS**

## COMPETENCY 12.0   DESIGN

### SKILL 12.1 Principles of Design in Textile Selection                 3.7%

Be sure to consider HARMONY-that's when the whole is achieved in a pleasing manner.  Second is PROPORTION-where size, length, and bulk relate to each other.  Third is BALANCE-where there is equal images at both ends from the center.  Fourth is RHYTHM-where the eye flows to all points of interest.  Fifth is EMPHASIS where you'll look to one image of the outfit and rest is the background.   Don't forget  thecomponentsofcolor,texture,print,andproportion.  Balance must be controlled in a fashion design.  Work with your figure.  Only put a bulky texture where you're thin, maybe a vest.  Line can give height if vertical.

### SKILL 12.2  Psychological Effects of Clothing Styles in Color, Line , and Design.

Color is the first thing people notice about an outfit.  Hue is the color.  Value is the lightness or  darkness of color.  Tints is if white is added.  Shades are if black is added to the hue. Intensity is the brightness of the hue.  Cool colors like green and blue make  the figure look smaller.  Hot colors like red, yellow, and orange  increase the size of the figure.  Line is the same as style.  They take your eye throughout the outfit. Lines can create illusions.  Design of an outfit  to fit   your  mood.  By simply changing a line in the design, it may change the look.

## COMPETENCY 13.0 TEXTILES                    2.1%

### SKILL 13.1  Textiles By Art Principles, Figure Types, Pattern Design, and Use.

Texture, the feel of the fabric is important for the results. It may be clinging, rough, smooth, stiff, or transparent. Always check the pattern for the garment for suggested fabrics for the design. Texture works with the color. Texture should carry out the theme of the occasion. There's no hatd set rule about mixing textures, colors, and lines. There must be unity and variety in the outfit. For the wardrobe you need a definite color-scheme. Things that mix and match. You keep this same color scheme for at least two years. Use basic colors like navy blue, gray, or brown. Color must be in balance. Proportion must be noticed. the colors must complement one and another. The size and proportion must fit the wearers figure type. Rougher fabrics seem bulkier than they are. Every design is a structure of lines and shapes. There's body lines, silhouette lines, and detail lines. Lines often make illusions in garments. Vertical lines make you look taller and thinner. Horizontal lines add width. Curves and diagonals lead the eye around. Proportion applies to space relationships within the design. Balance is equal interest on all sides of the outfit. Yet emphasis pulls your eye to one spot. Scale refers to size relationships. All design elements must work together. For figure types, there are short, average, and tall. Fall is the easiest to outfit.

### SKILL 13.2  Properties of Textiles in Relation to Use

See suggested fabrics on the pattern envelop when choosing material for a garment. Feel the fabric. Look at how it hangs. Elements of texture, how the light reflects showing dullness or sheen. Touch shows if the fabric is rough or smooth. Is the look rich or plain? What is the fabrics weight? Does it have body or drape? Texture and pattern design must work together. There needs to be balance in color as well. Color needs harmony.

### SKILL 13.3  Fibers, Yarns, Fabric Construction, Finishes, Wearability, and Durability.

Natural Fibers-from animals. Wool, cashmere, mohair, and alpaca. Natural fibers are warm and wrinkle free. It dyes well. If made with synthetic fibers added it pills. They should be dry cleaned. To iron use a press cloth and low temperature. Be careful not to preshrink. Silk is smooth and drapes well. It takes to dyes easily. Blends with synthetic or man-made fibers. Dry clean silk. Press on the wrong side with a medium iron. Silk is delicate. Be careful with pinning to cut out. There's a vegetable fiber. It's cotton. Cotton is strong. It blends well with other fibers. If it is treated to be crease-resistant, it doesn't need much ironing. It will shrink unless treated not to. Washable and can be ironed when damp. They can be treated with a wash and wear procedure.

Linen is cool and absorbent. It has a fresh finish. It blends with either manmade or animal made fabric. It will shrink. If sewing, shrink fabric first. The edges will ravel so finish with a zigzag stitch. Man-made fibers begin with rayon that is solution-dyed yarn giving color fast ability. Rayon drapes and dyes well. It blends easily. It can be craped or moireed. You can either wash or dry-clean. Do not wring it. Towel dried is the best. Acetate, also a man-made fiber. It is soft and smooth. It drapes easily. It dyes well. It can be blended with synthetic or natural fibers. It fades. It can be dry-cleaned or hand-washed. Use a cool iron and press while damp. Acrylic blends with natural or synthetics. Has warmth. Press carefully. Avoid sunlight and mildew. Washable. Iron at low setting. Sew with a fine needle. Nylon is a tough fabric. It blends well with all fabrics wash on a mild cycle. Polester is popular as a blend. It's wrinkle resistant and strong. It drapes well. Washes well in warm water. Wool blended with Dacron is washable. Cloth is either woven, knitted, or bond. There are a number of interesting finishes like drip0dry,crease-resistant, shrinkage - control,water-repellent,mothproofing,insulating,and color-fast processes.

## COMPETENCY 14.0 KNOWLEDGE OF CLOTHING WITH ACCESSORIES

2.1%

### SKILL 14.1 Cultural, Social, and Psychological Factors Influence Selection, Use, and Care of Clothing and Textile Products.

Cultural influences some group clothes. Example, Middle Eastern women cover their faces. Certain social occasions require specific styles of dress. For instance a bride and groom are very dressy. Going to the ball game, you dress casually. If you feel blue you put on your favorite slippers and a baggy sweater. Feeling on top of the world, put on your fancy red dress. How you feel effects how you dress. If you don't mind, you can buy all dry-clean only clothes. Knowing to separate your clothes for the laundry is valuable. Use Tide or Era or any detergent you desire. Liquid bleach is for the white loads. Use Clorax powder to brighten colors. Be sure to read the label of the clothes prior to washing.

### SKILL 14.2 Family Clothing Purchases

First of all there is a budget. Look for suitable clothes on the sale or clearance rack. Buy basic colors that will mix and match. Don't over buy. Purchase for the occasion. No need for a formal unless you are going to a prom. Buy your clothing under the rules or principles of art; harmony, proportion, balance, rhythm, and emphasis. Don't forget the elements of color either. Pick one strong hue to run your wardrobe color scheme. Texture like color effects the look of the garment. Use line to your advantage. Where vertical line adds height and makes one look thinner. Check the label on ready to wear to know laundry technique. Buying better clothing will last longer, especially if you need to hand down these clothes to more than one child.

### SKILL 14.3 Design Principles to Wardrobe Planning.

The effect of the fabric can create an illusion with use of line. There are so many tricks with stripes every year. Up and down stripes add height. A simple design will give the most pleasing results. Prints can also be used for various results in clothing. Prints make a figure look bigger. Darker colors decrease size. Often a person can pick a great style and line to flatter the figure; but ruin the effect by buying the wrong fabric to make it in. Texture decides how the material will feel. Is it rough or smooth, stiff or clinging. Shiny fabrics make you look larger. Dull fabrics make the person look smaller. Rough textured fabrics make the person look bigger because of bulkiness. Color helps add illusions to your wardrobe. Color can set the mood with your wardrobe. Hot colors like red add warmth. Dark colors absorb light and also add warmth.

Wear comfortable shorts and shirt to do daily chores. For work wear a simple dress, suit, skirt, or shirt. Keep them clean. For school wear mix and match separates. That's skirts, sweaters, jackets, shirts that mix up. A few basic dresses for social outings. Fill in your wardrobe for sports, traveling, and evenings out.

### SKILL 14.4 Quality Construction of Ready-made and Constructed Garments.

If you look at the ready to wear store bought clothes you see the seams pulling apart. Buttons and zippers are loose. Nothing was knotted. They won't last that long. Constructed garments show professionalism. Careful pressing between every step of construction gives you a professional look. Do one step at a time. Follow the instructions on your guide sheet. After the final completion of the garment, do the last pressing.

### SKILL 14.5 Custom-Made Garment vs.. Store-bought Garment

|       | Custom-Made          | Store-bought     |
|-------|----------------------|------------------|
| COST  | LOWER                | HIGHER           |
| FIT   | BETTER FOR YOUR BODY | NOT PERFECT      |
| STYLE | PERFECT-UNLIMITED    | LIMITED CHOICES  |

As you can see by the chart custom-made garments have three advantages over store-bought garments. Store-bought clothing may be low in cost, but they don't last as long as home construction. Thus they end up costing more in this throw away society. In store-bought clothes there's a limited supply to choose from.

### SKILL 14.6 Clothing Labels

Clothing labels are informative. They first tell the fabric type. Is it a blend? The size it is. The laundry instructions are invaluable on the label. Follow them carefully. If it states dry clean, don't wash and dry it. You'll just ruin it. The label tells the manufacturer if there's any problems with the garment. The label may tell where it was constructed. The other store label or tag will give the cost. The UPC bar code is here for check out.

### SKILL14.7 Rights and Responsibilities Concerning Clothing and Textile Purchases.

People need to purchase the proper size so it needn't be returned. If a return is necessary, bring it back in the bag with the receipt. It must be in the original condition. Don't keep it for months and then decide to take it back. People that open a package of socks for a size check and take a new package cost customers.

When items are shop lifted the cost goes back to us the consumer. These are the consumers responsibility. The consumer has the right to information. Ask any salesperson, if you have a question. And of course any consumer has the right to choose.

### SKILL 14.8  Use and Care of Clothing and Products by Values, Goals, Life Style, and Resources

Your lifestyle will help determine your clothing choices.  If your budget is restricted you can't afford dry cleaning.  So read the label for   laundry instructions.  Purchase the wash and wear.  If you want the garment to last, spend a bit more.  Check the clothing construction.  The better made  will last longer.  Remember to purchase a basic colorsceme.  Get a few pieces to mix and match.  Remember if your lifestyle is on the run, to buy easy to wear and wash clothes.

### SKILL 14.9  Legislative Influences On The Textile And  Clothing Industries

Congress has helped the seamstress and tailor in the ready to wear industry, by making laws to pay better.  They used to care the factories, sweatshops.  There was little air and dirty conditions to work in.  Many of the workers came down with tuberculoses.   There wasn't health insurance for the workers.  Congress forced factory owners to better the conditions.   Laws have been passed to improve conditions in the textile and apparel industries.

## COMPETENCY 15.0   CLOTHING AND TEXTILE PRODUCTION AND MAINTENANCE .                    2.1%

### SKILL 15.1  Guidances For Selection, Care, and Use of Sewing Machines.

There are many sewing machines to pick from today.  They can do, many specialized stitches.  There's an amazing variety of makes, model, and prices.  The manufacturers keep pace with new fabrics, fashion, sewing, and items to fit everyone's needs and skills.  When you buy  a  sewing machine don't spend more than you need.  There's three types of sewing machines.  The straight stitch, zigzag stitch, and automatic stitch.  Buy only what you need.  Comparison shop.  Get a demonstration of the sewing machine.  Try out the machine too.  Find out what accessories. are included with your model.  Learn how to thread your machine, replace the needle correctly, and wind the bobbin.  Be sure to control the thread tension.  This controls the seams.  Don't spend more than you have to.

### SKILL 15.2  Guidelines for Use of Small Sewing Equipment

Needles come in sizes 9(for delicate fabrics) to 18(for heavy fabric).  See pattern guide to know size of needle for garment's fabric.  Look under notions.  There are ball-point needles for lingerie or elastic.  There are double needles for pattern stitching. Bobbins are metal or plastic.  Have several colors ready.  Keep extra bobbins available.  You need a few tools by your machine.  You need a tiny brush for lint removal.  A small screwdriver like used to tighten glasses.  You need sewing machine oil.  Do  not over buy sewing equipment.

There are several feet for the sewing machine.  Zipper fit to sew on a zipper and get close to the teeth.  There's a hemming foot, gathering foot, roller foot, and button foot.

### SKILL 15.3  Use and Care of Laundry and Pressing Equipment

When it comes to laundry, follow the label on one garment.  If you made the garment, remember the fabric type and wash accordingly.  So separate clothes into whites which you'll bleach and darks.  You should separate fabric types after color separating.  Be careful adding in one cup of detergent and one cup of bleach for the colors.  Fold after drying.  Use the correct cycle when washing.

Pressing equipment help throughout the construction of the garment.  Press as you sew and the garment will look professional.  Get a good iron that has a steam button.  You need an ironing board.  It should be sturdy with a pad covering the board.  Press clothes are similar in weight to the fabric you're using.  Have at least two ready for use.  A tailor's ham is a stuffed cushion.  It is used to press curved areas like darts, sleeve caps, and any rounded shape.  Press mitts fit over your hand and are used on small hard to reach areas.  A sleeve board is two little ironing boards hooked together one on top of  the other.  There's a seam roll that is long tubular stuffed cushion. It's used to press long seams like in a sleeve. You can make your own sleeve board by rolling up a magazine with fabric scraps. Pressing board. It helps you press points, curves, and straight edges. There are pressing pads that four fabrics stitched together. Some people have a clapper. It's a block of wood used with steam to flatten seams. Woolens and linens are two fabrics that are hard to press. This clapper helps the seams lay flat.

## SKILL 15.4  Pattern Selection

Patterns must be picked by figure type and accurate body measurements. Take your bust, waist, and hip measurements. Take all these measurements; bust, waist, hip, neck to waist, shoulders, arm length, neck and arm circumference, and skirt length. Look on the back of the pattern and buy the one that your measurements match up with. For women choose patterns from Misses, Women's, and Half-sizes. Most patterns are bought by bust size. Use your waist measurement to buy a skirt, slacks, or shorts pattern.

## SKILL 15.5  Preparation of Fabrics

Be careful, the success of your sewing depends on your fabric. Feel the fabrics weight, bulk, and texture. Is it wrinkle resistant? Will it stretch? Is the color good for you? If you're ready to begin,f old the straighten and pressed fabric as seen on the layout diagram. You need to cut and tear on the edge of the fabric. This will get it on grain. Be sure you've folded on the lengthwise grain. Usually the fabric is washed and dried first. Then straighten the grain.

## SKILL 15.6  Pattern Alterations for Differences Between Pattern Size and Body Measurements

All alterations should be done on the pattern. Machine baste the garment pieces together to check size before permanent stitching. Machine baste shoulder seams, underarm seams, and front and back seams of the garment.

On the printed pattern piece you'll find double lines indicating this is where to cut the tissue pattern piece too lengthen or shorten. Be sure to follow the grainline arrows. Notches must be cut around outward. But some patterns come with three different sizes on one tissue piece. This allows you to use the larger sizes top with the smaller size bottom.

### SKILL 15.7 Order of Constructing a Garment

First wash and dry the fabric. Pick the layout from bolt width and which view you are sewing. Use a tracing wheel and paper to transfer markings, like darts or pockets onto the fabric. Cut carefully with sharp scissors. Be sure to go around notches. Press pieces before pinning to fabric. Lay on fabric just like picture in the guide. Follow through step by step as the guide instructs. Press after each step. Be certain to choose fabric that is listed on the pattern envelop for suggested fabrics. Check the notions listed and get them. If you don't use a suggested fabric the garment may not drape as desired.

### SKILL 15.8 Evaluation of Constructed Garments

First is the garment sewn well? Will the seams come apart? If plaids, do they match? Do all closures work? Now, does it fit well? Is the zipper straight and secure? Are the raw edges of the inseam raveling? If so you can close them with seam binding or seam tape. Are the inside edges of the facings finished? If not you can zigzag stitch around the edge.

### SKILL 15.9 Fit for Men, Women, and Children of a Pattern or a Garment and Some Alteration Ideas

Both to shorten or lengthen cut on the double black line of the pattern piece. Space apart to lengthen. Overlap to shorten. This is for the sleeves or bodice as well. You can raise the hipline by folding up the pattern piece. For a skirt you can cut off unneeded length at the bottom. To change the waistline you can redraw seamlines. Necklines maybe gaping and easily pulled up. Shoulders may be sloping, square, narrow, or broad. These are easy alterations.

### SKILL15.10 Alteration Methods

First you can do alterations with the pattern piece. In order to alter, you need to transfer the markings from the pattern to the fabric. Be sure to mark on the wrong side of the fabric. Transfer seamlines, fold line, darts, center front, and center back, and grainlines.

You can transfer pattern symbols to the fabric with tailor's tacks. That's a few stitches with a different color of thread than the fabric wherever the symbols are. You can use tailor's chalk too.

The best method of correcting size is in the pattern pieces. Next you can simply alter after completion according to the guide sheet. You can baste the garment together and check for fit. Make the corrections and then make the final sewing and pressing.

### SKILL 15.11 Recycled Garments Considering Fabric, Design, Time, and Cost

To recycle a garment use a strong fabric. Little time is used in construction. In the 70's it was popular to cut old long or short jeans and cut and realign to be a skirt and then sewed it up. The cost should be terrifically low since you're redoing your old clothes. It's also a means of income to put your old decent clothes into a consignment shop. When it's sold they send you money.

### SKILL 15.12 Common Clothing Repairs

It's a good idea to be able to sew on a button. Bring thread up from the bottom of fabric. Secure the button with a shank. Learn to hem a garment too. There's several hemming stitches. There are many hems; plain, eased, circular, and narrow. Learn at least one. If a seam starts coming apart, knot the thread and sew it closed.

### SKILL 15.13 Laundering and Pressing Certain Fabrics

Wool should be dry-cleaned. Use a press cloth and moderate iron. Silk is to be dry-cleaned too. Press it on the wrong side with a moderate iron. Cotton shrinks. It is washable and can be pressed with a hot iron while damp. There are treated cottons too. They are wash and wear and need little ironing. Linen is a cool fabric with a crisp look. It is washable. Press linen with a hot iron on the wrong side. Shrink before cutting fabric. Rayon is to be dry-cleaned. Use it with a warm iron. Do not wrinkle. Acrylic is a washable blend. Use only a low setting iron. Polyester washes in warm water. It needs no ironing. It does not shrink.

### SKILL 15.14 Stain Removal

Treat any stain right away. If the fabric is thin or loosely woven, pce the stain inside out in a small bowl of cleaner, like Era or Tide. Rinse, let dry, now launder or dry-clean. If the fabric is thick or firmly woven, dampen the stain with a sponge moistened in solvent or cleaner. Work from the center of the stain to the edge. For a hardened stain place a dampened pad with detergent on it. For a greasy stain if it is washable regular laundry with Shout It Out should remove it. A non-greasy stain on a washable article needs to be soaked for thirty minutes or longer. Then put through the regular cycle in the washing machine. If the stain is alcohol, and the garment is washable, soak it in cold water. Then wash in warm water and rinse. If it's still there soak the garment in peroxide and water mixed. Pen marks can be soaked in detergent with warm water. Or take it to the dry cleaners. Gum needs to have ice on the gum. Then chip it off with a butter knife. Now soak it in cleaning fluid. Cosmetics are removed with a presoak or Shout It Out in the load. Perspiration spots need to be sponged off with ammonia or white vinegar. Next launder normally.

HOME ECONOMICS

### SKILL15.15  Storing Garments

If something is dry-cleaned simply hang it up.  If the items are washed weekly, fold properly, and put away in the  dresser.  Brides like to preserve their bridal gowns professionally.  Send  the gown to the dry cleaners and have it boxed and sealed.   The air is what deteriorates the fabric.  If you want your offspring to wear your bridal gown, have it restored.

## COMPETENCY 16.0   GROOMING AND  APPEARANCE.         2%

### SKILL 16.1  Grooming and Appearance

Take care of yourself.  A healthy person looks better.  Wash daily and brush your teeth three times.  Bathe or shower every other day.  Deodorant is used daily.  Grooming includes combing your hair.  Keeping  it trimmed.  Ladies use makeup sparingly.  Wear clean clothes.  It doesn't take loads of money to keep one's appearance clean and mannerly.  Present yourself in the best manner possible.  Dress for the occasion.  Casual to  a ball game  and formal to the prom.

## COMPETENCY 17.0  AMERICAN ECONOMIC SYSTEM
3.1%

### SKILL  17.1  American Economics and the Consumer

The  United States Economic System is based on the value of the dollar. You can follow if it is a good economic year or not with the indexes on wall street with the stocks and bonds.  Money is made during wars.  This is a time of peace. Businesses must struggle to make a profit.  There is inflation when things are priced higher than they're worth.  But the entire democratic free enterprise theme is based on supply and demand.   That means if the supply  is limited, the price will be driven up.  If the supply is overflowing the demand not so great, the price will drop.  This works wherever the consumers are free to choose.

### SKILL 17.2  Pricing, Production Distribution, and Selling Goods and
### Services.

As I mentioned before the price will change according to supply and demand. If there is a large supply, the price will be low.  If the supply is small, the demand high, and the price goes up.  Production costs of the raw materials and the man power set the items original price.  Then the wholesaler  that buys from the factory doubles the price to the retailer.  The retailer raises the cost three times to the consumer.  In the middle is the distributor that makes the delivery of the items throughout the United States.  Of course, the distributor gets their cut of the profit.  So selling goods and services the seller always gets his money.  He does this buy charging more than he bought it for.  The only control consumers have in the open market is not to buy inferior products. So no matter how low the price drops, it won't get sold.

## SKILL 17.3  Taxation on Local, State, and National Levels-the Purposes, Functions, and Sources

There are several ways Americans pat taxes. We pay income tax in April. A percentage of your annual salary is turned over to the government. Then there are taxes on consumables-food and gas. Right now Florida has a 6 % tax on food. Then in some counties like Palm Beach there's an additional 6% gas tax. The gas bought in Palm Beach is higher in price than in other Florida counties. Taxes on gas in San Francisco, California are 30% ,so gas costs around $1.68/gal. while Boca Raton, Florida pay $1.32.

The taxes are important. The money collected helps the people. Welfare and food stamps are funded by taxes. The roads and bridges use the tax money repaired. Also to build new ones. There are tax paid daycare for those below poverty level. That's daycare for the preschooler and the elderly. The schools receive some tax money. Not much since the lottery claims to give big bucks to education. But the lottery cuts back yearly on what money goes to the schools.

## SKILL 17.4 Government, Producers, Sellers, Families, and the economy.

Governments protect the consumer by inspecting products to be sure they are safe. Government tries to be sure working conditions for employees. What happens is the producers are regulated by government safety restrictions. Sellers then are limited to how high of cost for the item by what people are willing to pay and by what the producer sold it for originally. Families in the economy can buy or not buy. That's their choice. But families are controlled in the market place by the sellers price. Again the seller is controlled by the producer. The producer must answer to the government. There are definite demands on the interrelationships of the government producers, sellers, families, and the economy.

## SKILL 18.0 CONSUMER CHOICES                                    3.1%

### SKILL 18.1 Families Consumption by Income.

Most American families live above their income. What I mean if the household income is $45,000 and they spend $50,000. How is this possible? Most Americans have credit cards where they buy now and pay later. Added on is an interest charge. Poverty level is around $10,000 income for the family. But at any end of the income scale, the family spends all they can.

### SKILL 18.2 Consumer Choices are Related to Cultural Background, Socioeconomic Situation, Stage in the Life Cycle, and Lifestyle.

Consumers have many different choices. If you are raised Italian you pick spaghetti and pizza. If you are Israeli ,you might eat blintzes and gefilte fish. Your cultural background controls your choices. Your socioeconomic level and lifestyle on the upper end of the economic scale demands you spend more to keep up with your clique. You know 'Keep up with the Jones'. If your at the start of the lifecycle with marriage you need a budget. Then you have a baby which promotes many costs. As children grow so do other costs. When the children are grown they launch off to college, the army, or trade school. Now the cost is high if the children are in college. Otherwise the empty nest of mom and dad has some extra money for them to enjoy or save for the golden retirement years. Lifestyle is where you buy certain items to fit your ways and means. If your a doctor, your car costs over $25,000 and you belong to the local golf country club . If you're a bus driver and your wife stays at home with the little ones, your income is low. You have enough money for the basics only, food, shelter, and clothing. No frills, but everyone is close in this family and happy.

### SKILL 18.3 Family Financial Decisions Influences by Personal Standards During the Life cycle

Let's start out as newlyweds. At this stage of the life cycle the two are trying to sort out their mutual standards. Once they are established, they can set up a savings as well as a budget. From these all the family, financial decisions can be sided. As soon as the baby is born the financial decisions change in this second stage of the life cycle. The couple may start, a college fund for the baby depending on the family's standards. Now the children are in the school age level of the life cycle. This requires many finances at this level. After school age children comes the launching years of the life cycle. Children marry, go to college, start a career, go to the armed forces. This should be a time for a little extra cash for the working parent couple. Last is retirement; when there is no income. Hopefully your pension and social security will be enough financial support to live a comfortable life.

## SKILL 18.4  Resource Factors that Influence Consumer Choices

Of course, how much money you have will influence what you buy, what you can afford.  With fruit and vegetables, some areas of the country, Florida and California, have fresh produce all year round.  Then in the North they can only get the fresh produce during the summer.  Availability with supply and demand determine cost of products.  If you don't have time to shop buy out of a catalog.  Mail shopping is convenient.  If you don't have storage room, don't buy it.  Say you love the side-by-side double door.  Refrigerator, but it can't fit in your kitchen.  You may be better off with the smaller refrigerator with the freezer on top.  Then buy a small freezer for the garage.  Knowledge is the easiest resource to multiply.  Do a bit of comparison shopping before any purchase.  Then you'll know more about the product of interest.

## SKILL 18.5  Goals By Availability and Utilization of Resources

Realizing  your goals, but remember the availability of area resources and proper use.  If your goal  is to bake and sell apple  pies, yet there's nowhere to get apples.  Then you have to  buy canned apple pie filling or give up your idea.  Make your goal realistic by what is usable in the area.  If you are to produce anything, you need the resources to do it.

## SKILL 18.6  Advertising to Selling to the Consumer Advertising is Charged by the Manufacturer on the Product They're Selling

Yet advertising brings customers  to buy that item advertised.  So even if the cost of advertising  is allot it doesn't matter.  Advertising gets the consumer to the  shop.  Advertising brings in the business.  The cost of the item is raised up too cover what the manufacturers put out for the advertising.  People want to believe the advertising.  Advertising influences you to see the item advertised.

## SKILL 18.7  Advertising-Accurate Information that's Realistic, and Appropriate for it's Audience.

Often times advertising is exaggerated.  The consumer needs to think  is it honest?  Is the information realistic?  Is it aimed at a specific audience?  The government reprimands any untruthful advertisement companies.  Be careful when advertising to aim at the right audience or age group. The information you try to sell must be accurate.  Be certain you already tested the product.

## COMPETENCY 19.0 MONEY MANAGEMENT

### SKILL 19.1 Income and Expenses

The main rule to remember is that your income needs to be larger than your expenses. This is how you run a budget. List all you spend for one or two weeks You have a spending record. You know what money you make at work. Sure some goes into the bank as a savings for emergencies. Look over your spending record to locate places you could lower your expenses. Then be sure you can have extra money left over after your expenses are met. This is your payment or extra banking savings. Don't over extend yourself with credit cards.

### SKILL 19.2 Budget

There are fixed and non-fixed expenses. You have to start off with a budget. Here you start at the top with the income and subtract necessary payments. Fixed expenses are the mortgage or rent. Car payments stay the same monthly. Insurance remains the same. Bills like the electric, water, doctor's, and gas for the car, vary weekly and are non-fixed bills. The only way to make a dent in your budget is to lower a fixed payment. Remember to include paying yourself. Keep a savings account for future emergencies as well as for large purchases like a car, vacation, or refrigerator. Don't work for your bills only. Keep yourself in the swing with lots of green. Remember in a marriage a budget includes two incomes combined. But two must agree on how much goes to each bill.

### SKILL 19.3 Record-Keeping System

With your budget have a bill paying system. You may have an incoming basket of bills and the outgoing bills that have been written and recorded in your checkbook. They just need to be stamped. Keep the registrar of your checkbook accurate. Write in deposits and withdrawals. Subtract after each check is written. Both partners in a marriage should enter their deposits in the check registrar. It's easiest to write checks to the bill companies and remember to subtract all checks. Add in all deposits. Both partners should know how the finances are recorded in case something happens to one of them.

### SKILL 19.4 Establishing, Using, and Protecting , Credit

To establish credit start with a checking and/or savings account. Go to the bank of your choice. To open either account, you need to put in $25-$50. As soon as you start banking, keep accurate records. If you use credit wisely, you'll always be able to get it. If you mess up, it will be extremely difficult to get bank services later.

To use a savings account simply put part of your check into your account. Use a deposit slip. You can also take out money with a withdrawal slip. Try not to. The more in the account the more financially set you will be. Have direct deposit if possible. The employer takes out your specified amount of money and put it in your savings account from each paycheck. I know some companies let you deduct money from the employees check for a tax annuity. This lowers the annual income from the employees salary by the amount of the tax annuity. You pay taxes on the reduced salary amount. If you don't watch your money, you won't have it.

### SKILL 19.5 Credit, Availability, and Cost.

There's many different types of credit. You can get store credit cards with 19%interest on each dollar spent. There's bank credit cards that have lower interest cost, like 6.5% first six months and then back up to 12%-17% interest after that. It's best to buy with cash having no interest to pay. If you can't afford something with cash wait to buy it. As far as availability, there's many credit cards to choose from. Banks also have many loans for cars, houses, boats, and vacations. You need good credentials to get any loan from a bank. There's several things a bank considers when loaning money. First is the one wanting a loan vested in a job? If the loan is a mortgage, the house is the collateral. If it's for a car, the car is the collateral. Banks want to loan to people with careers-collateral-character. Character means with three references that state that you are a good credit risk. They say you are honest, hard working, and deserving.

### SKILL 19.6 Credit Contract-Borrower and Lender

The borrower must repay the loan with interest by the stipulations in the contract they signed. If they become a miss with the payments, the item on credit is repossessed. The borrower when filling out the application and loan forms must be honest. All information must be truthful. The lender gives the money to the buyer. Buyer gives it to the car dealer or house seller. Now the borrower makes monthly payments to the lender, the bank.

### SKILL 19.7 Different Financial Institutions

There is the main commercial bank where you have savings, checking, mortgage loans, car loans, and even business loans. There where majority of the banking needs you have are handled. There are a simple savings and loan banks. They don't handle checking and savings accounts. There are credit unions, which are owned by the members involved. Like a teacher's credit union or a federal employees credit union. There are lower interest rates on loans in the credit union. You can have a checking, savings, car or house loan, and a business loan from your credit union too.

## SKILL 19.8 Insurance, Benefits, and Coverage

As far as benefits are concerned, look at your job salary. Does the benefits round it out? In teaching I get family, health, dental, and eye insurance. I get life insurances disability if I'm injured on the job. My life insurance is $100,000 and the spouse is $10,000 and each of my boys have $5,000. My health insurance is taken from my paycheck two times a month. But when we go to the doctors it's copayment, which is low enough. For medication at Eckerds or Wallgreens it's only $3 per presciption. Dental is like a doctor visit, a $10 copayment. There's two free claddings yearly at the dentist too. The eye coverage is 20% we pay for our families. For an unknown reason there is no eye coverage for the employee. The HOMO pays 80% of the family eye care visit. Another benefit at work is payroll deduction to a savings account in the credit unions. Not seeing all my money makes it easier to save. I have another benefit from my job. I have payroll deduction to a tax annuity. An annuity builds up quickly. You can't remove any of the money without a penalty. It's interest is higher because you guarantee the bank will be there for a year.

## SKILL 19.9 Family Benefits by Social Security, Retirement, and Estate Planning

If you work in America some of your money comes from your paycheck into your Social Security fund. When you retire you will get a monthly amount from the government based on your last ten working years salaries. Unfortunately if your husband worked, paid into social security and dies, his wife will receive his social security money to support the children. There are many retirement homes and programs jumping up throughout the United States. The government pays a little into the retirement programs. If you have help in middle age too plan out your golden years estate planning. Be sure you do it. Know a place of reasonable rates. Look for medical help on the premises.

## COMPETENCY 20.0 CONSUMERISM

### SKILL 20.1 Buy from Stores, Catalogs, and Media Services

Being able to get out to a variety of stores gives you the best selection. Most stores take cash, checks, and credit cards. With a catalog, you can't try on to check the fit. Buy by catalog if bad weather like the winter's up North keep you from getting to the store. Then what you ordered can be delivered to you house. If you purchase off of QVC, the buying channel on the television, you can see what you are ordering. QVC lets you break up the total cost into 3-4 payments.

### SKILL 20.2 Products-Standards, Warranty, Use, Care, and Cost

Whenever you go to buy anything, a car, clothes, or a Sega game, do you know if you're getting a good deal? Be sure to check for a Good Housekeeping Seal or the UL seal saying these products have been tested and are up to par. Look for a full warranty or at least a partial warranty, so if there is any problems the manufacturer can repair it at little or no cost. If it's only a partial warranty what does it cover? Are there directions to show you proper use. Care is common sense not to drop it or force it. Read the instructions. When it comes to cost, check neighboring or similar stores. See who has the best price. Usually you pay for what you get. If it's a $200 radio against the sound from a $125 radio. The higher price has more to offer. Standards are always important. Don't purchase junk, thar's the only way we can get them off the market.

### SKILL 20.3 Purchasing Guidelines

First when it's time to buy something, do you just runoff to your favorite closest store and without a blink buy it? Yoooou should research first. Check the Sunday Newspaper flyers for the best cost and standards. You never should go over your budget. Anytime the purchase is over$50 the family must discuss it. Guidelines to shopping say pay cash or walk away. Avoid using credit cards. When you know you need it, find the best fit for the lowest cost.

### SKILL 20.4 Wise Shopping Guidelines

When you shop stick to your list. Impulse buying can waste your cash. When you set a limit for how much you will spend on school clothes or how much you will spend at Christmas on gifts stick to your limit. Look at clearance and sale racks. Don't buy it unless it fits you and your wardrobe. Limit yourself to a dollar amount, not to exceed every month for shopping.

## SKILL 20.5 Consumer Rights and Responsibilities

Consumers have the right to information. Thus we have the right to choose. We have the right to redress, which is to complain and get fixed inferior merchandise. We as consumers must notify producers of poor quality products. We have the right to safe products. We must demand top notch products on the market place. Warranties are necessary with products being sold. If people are good consumers that do not shoplift or do not open merchandise in the store and not buy it, then the cost of this negligence can not be passed back down to the consumer. Believe me any wrong doing in the marketplace gets put back on to the consumer.

## SKILL 20.6 Consumers to Help Public Policy Relating to Consumer Concerns.

Numbers is still the way to change city hall. Anything like a stop sign where it's not needed, start with a petition. Get lots of neighbors and any big wigs you know to sign it too. Go to City Hall when you have a petition of 50-500 names. Show City Hall you mean business. If you get on a city committee you can make a big difference. When the Commissioner asks for volunteers for the committee volunteer your own time. Make a real difference in your city government. Listen to your neighbors at the grocery store, at the pickup line for your kids at school, while at the skate rink, at church, or in any store. Take what your neighbors want and work to get it through city government. Then you've really done something.

## SKILL 20.7 Laws and Regulations to Protect the Consumer

The government can at any time require the removal of anything off any store counter. Food and Drug Administration is a government agency to do the removal like the Tylenol scare where cyanide was found in the capsules. All Tylenol was called off the shelves. When the FBI settled the case and arrested the bad guy the good Tylenol went back on the shelf. The EPA-Environmental Protection Agency checks to see factories exhaust stay within lawful limits. There are local laws to fight pollution. People like Rralph Nadar fight for the little man against big business. Ralph Nadar was able to convince Congress that the Pinto and the Chevette were too small and unsafe. There are many safeguards for the consumer.

### SKILL 20.8 Consumer Rights and Responsibilities, Major Legislation Relating to Consumers, Warranties and Guarantees, Deceptive Practices, Methods of Recourse, Consumer Protection Agencies and Services.

The government tries to stay on top of all fraudulent business practices. People should watch for their guaranty and warranty. Call the Better Business Bureau if you think you are being taken an advantage of or to see if the business is legitimate. What can a consumer do if they are taken advantage of? They can go to small claims court for problems up to $200. Let's say you have a car you bought and it's a lemon, contact a lawyer of the public. Just call the courthouse. Consumers can first complain to a store for a rotten product nicely and show the receipt. There are public defenders and other agencies to help the consumer being taken advantage of. To help yourself contact the television channel to expose the rotten product and the store that won't take it back. Go to the public for help when you can't afford a private attorney to deal with your outrage.

**HOME ECONOMICS**

## COMPETENCY 21.0 RESOURCE MANAGEMENT

3.1%

### SKILL 21.1 Management Principles and Techniques

You need to start off with a budget to run your monetary resources. Use the decision making steps for situations. First identify the problem. Next choose the alternative from all your possible alternatives to solve the situation. Choose the alternative that looks like it will handle the situation. Do the PLAN. Last evaluate the plan used. On your budget set up the fixed expenses. Then list your expenses that change every month. Is there any fixed payment that you can lower? That's how to help lower your budget. Have more money than you spend. A great technique to use is spend less than you make. Always pay yourself first. Have a savings account. Put money into your savings account weekly. Don't buy more than you can afford. Supply and demand still run the pricing of the free market. United States runs on the open market. Many goods are high in supply, thus the price will be low. If the demand for the product is very high, and there is a little supply, the cost will sky rocket. Thus people in business hope to use very few resources. As little labor as possible too. Get this product out to the people. Low budget advertising along with small principles and techniques will most likely end up with a huge profit.

### SKILL 21.2 Resource Management

Resources are not unlimited. There is so much water, so much trees, and only so much land. Humans can not overuse the resources left on the earth. Mankind must conserve the allotted resources. If a resource becomes scarce take care of it. That's when gasoline was rationed to consumers. Be sure to put your extra cash into a bank account in order to gain a little interest. Your lifestyle and joint in the life cycle will influence your use of money.

### SKILL 21.3 Resource Conservation

The EPA-environmental protection agency helps when areas need to be declared endangered. Often times areas of the United States are called National Parks. Some natural resources must be preserved, not wasted. This same part of the government protects many areas of the land that are too beautiful to let it go. Most of the conservation is government controlled thanks to President Hoover. The government is permitted to save lands in there natural state throughout the USA.

### SKILL 21.4 Household Cleaning, Sanitation, Maintenance, and Repairs

Tidy up clutter like clothes or toys around daily. Weekly the house must be dusted, swept, mopped, and vacuumed. Do the laundry once or twice a week. Then during spring and fall cleaning turn the mattresses. Clean the closets. Throw out allot. Have the comforters or bedspreads dry-cleaned. Once a year have the carpets steam cleaned by a company or rent a wet vac to shampoo your carpeting yourself. Keep up on your house painting about once every four or five years inside or out. Or else try wallpaper. A border of wallpaper looks terrific on a painted room. If you keep up on your cleaning inside and out around the house, you'll have a sanitary home.

When it comes to maintenance keep everything in working order. If you can fix it call a handy man or someone who can. Repairs are the same. Keep things in working order. If you can't fix it when it breaks, call someone to take care of it.

## COMPETENCY 22.0  HOUSING SELECTION          3.1%

### SKILL 22.1 Housing Industry is Related to the Economic, Welfare of the Nation

The state of the nations economy sets the T-Bill which home loans are based on. If it goes up loans go up and vice versa. If the T-Bill goes high up many will have to quit buying because loans and prices will go up. When people stop buying due to high loan rates the housing industry builds less. It's an overall shut down of a major system of the United States. When money is spent in the housing industry the interest rates come down and more buying gets going. Buying and selling is the main idea.

### SKILL 22.2 Housing Trends

As more  people try to move into a specific area, the developer gets more houses built. The people leave the city for their dream home in suburbia. This promotes many different styles of homes. Parks and schools sprout up. Then up go the grocery stores and restaurants. Home Depot goes up, doctor's offices, fire stations, police, and malls open up. The public gets what they need like community pools and hospitals. It does take two salaries to own a nice house in suburbia. The trend is to get your own house when you're married. They are so expensive. Some people luck out and the parents or inlays help contribute to the children's house, down payment. To rent is almost as high as a mortgage payment. Then it's impossible to save for a down payment.

With the demise of the family in America, there are many routine family lifestyle disappearing and alternate homelifes  appearing. There is an increase in the need of apartments  or condos for two incomes professionally. They don't always wish to own any property. This means less need to build.  Yet the affluent are still owning several residences.  Currently Florida, Colorado, California, and Texas are on top of the list of popular places where building many homes are taking  place. This shows that where the people want housing this is where  developers will build. Will it be a fair price? Who's to say? The middle class seems the most  stressed at holding on. The upper crust have no problem buying houses. Even the  lower class can go into  public housing. If a large group of handicapped people were expected to move into an area housing accommodating the handicapped would be constructed. The government would see to it. When all that was needed for the Olympics  in Atlanta, Georgia, it was built.  Dorm  work, housing, and all.  Fortunately the homeless even have shelters. Whatever the population  desires affects the housing selections.

## SKILL 22.3  Housing Developments-Regulated by the Government

Your very near the poverty line of $10,000.  If you live in a public housing development.  HUD-Hoousing Urban Development is a government agency that builds Public Housing.  HUD decides who gets which apartment.  In order to qualify for public welfare housing not only are you working for almost nothing, you have no access to credit.  You barely can pay what bills you have and you have nothing overdue.  No bad credit.  The government wants you working, putting your babies in a government-no pay- daycare.  Of course, you have food stamps.  With all this government help, why work?  Well soon you won't get welfare housing or foodstuffs.  That's is up to President  Clifton.(1996).

## SKILL 22.4  Types of Housing

There are apartments.  That's a community hooked together four to eight units.  There's a shared playground,  pool, and laundry facility.  Condos where they are owned individually, but still hooked together and very much like apartments.  Townhouses maybe hooked together, but are always up and down and hooked together.  They may be hooked to another villa, which is a one floor apartment that you own and are attached to one other dwelling.  Duplexes are hooked together with only one common wall.  The best is an individual dwelling.  Your own house attached to no one else.  You may have a community area with a pool, tennis courts, and a basketball court for the young at heart.  What's best for you is where you should live.  Is it a cabin in North Carolina?  Or a Domecenter in Texas?  All houses need a kitchen for food storage and preparation.  There's a need for bedrooms for sleeping, clothes hanging in a closet, an eating area in the kitchen or else formally in the dining room. Bathrooms with showers, baths, and jacuzz.  A living room and a laundry room. There must be a fair sized garage.  When you  can afford all the fancy conveniences of wealth, you'll probably have a pool.

## SKILL 22.5  Housing Selections

The area you live in is dependant on the local schools, if you have children. Then you find a residence within your means.  If you have to consider cost, location, size, and square footage you'll pick a great location.  The price of your new home will be perfect.  So schools, location, size, cost, and extras determine which house you'll buy.  Do you have good credit?  Let's get a mortgage set up with a down payment.  Do you show good credit use?  Then you're all set.

## SKILL 22.6  Lease and Mortgage Sales Contracts

A lease is a legal agreement between the renter and the owner.  If you rent or lease, all that you pay monthly goes to the owner to pay the mortgage.  He may pay other bills for the property too.  When it's a lease you are the landlord.  If it's a mortgage at the end of fifteen or thirty years you are the owner.  It's best if you have decent acceptable credit to buy and pay off a mortgage. Basically a standard lease gets you onto a property. There is little put as a down payment. But the property may be lease option to buy. This way whatever you put up for the down payment and all the previous rent payments are put towards the selling price.

### SKILL 22.6 Standard Lease and Mortgage Sales Contract

A Standard lease gets you into a property with little for a down payment. Usually money equal to first and last months rent are used to get an apartment with a standard lease. A standard lease states the date you took over the apartment. It lasts for one year. It shows that appliances breaking down will be fixed by the landlord. It tells the common grounds and pool. The basic rules of the complex are in the leases.

The mortgage sales contract is a legal binding document with the details for selling a house. How much down payment is required? That's about 20% of the selling price. When will the house be vacated? When can you move in? What upgrades in the house will be written into the contract to remain in the house? When will the roof be checked? The mortgage sales contract gets the buyer in and the seller out. It's that legal binding that makes the house sale work.

### SKILL 22.7 Renting Verses House Buying

The best part of renting is when your lease is over you can easily move. But rents are almost as high as mortgages. If you just move into an area it's good to rent first until you know what school district and area you want to buy in. Be sure to pay your rent on time. It will be a sign of good credit. That's proof when you decide to go for a mortgage and buy a house. It's better to pay your monthly houses payment for a reason. You want to get to the day fifteen or thirty years from now down the road you'll own your house outright. You'll be able to live on your pension since you won't have that larger mortgage to cover. When owning a house, there are tax advantages.

### SKILL 22.8 Cost of Housing Needs

All household costs must be covered in the family budget. There are many hidden maintenance costs. Keep your air conditioner costs. Keep your air conditioner in a good working condition. Same for all of your appliances. Keep them in good working condition. The cost to replace an air conditioner or refrigerator is in the thousands. According to the government 31% of the United States budget is spent yearly on housing. Remember that housing for the poverty stricken. Even up to the rich, there must be a budget. Budget is based on household income. Your wants and needs are influenced by your values. Fixed spending payments are the same monthly. These are the required bills like mortgage, utilities-electricity and or gas, water bill, food is not the same, it is flexible payment, one that changes each month. Phone bills are flexible. Fixed would be on a car loan. Monthly let's say the mortgage runs about $700. Then the car payment is $400 for two cars each month. Elasticity is near $170 in the summer. In winter the electricity runs about $80. No air conditioning needed. The water and garbage pickup runs $25/ month. Add the newspaper for $20/6 months. The phone bill runs $30/ month. The food monthly runs as high as $400/month. $1820 per month, is a high amount to pay every month. You'd need a $20,000 income at least. Remember what you want and need to spend money on. Childcare, health insurance, and entertainment costs haven't even been figured into this monthly payment.

## COMPETENCY 23.0  HOME CONSTRUCTION                    3.1%

### SKILL 23.1  Kitchen Work Areas for Family Needs

You need several work areas in a kitchen.  Establish a washing work area where you have a 3 section sink, wash, rinse, and sanitize pots and pans or dishes and glasses.  There are four major kitchen work areas or work centers.  One is with the refrigerator-freezer center for food storage.  Here the counter space is close to be used for loading and unloading.  Storage space is available for items used when serving refrigerator or frozen food. The range center is a gas or electric range.  A microwave oven may be included.  You need at least one side counter space.  Storage is needed for foods to use, stored in the refrigerator-freezer. Range center is a gas or electric range.  A microwave oven may be included .  You need at least one side counter space.   Storage is needed for foods to use stored pots, pans, cooking tools, like ladles, wooden spoons for stirring, turners, and pot holders. Sink or cleanup center  is needed with surrounding appliances like the dishwasher, food waste disposal, and a trash compactor.  Cleanup includes washing dishes and utensils and cleaning fruits, vegetables, and other foods.  There should be adequate counter space for stacking dishes.  Storage space is necessary for coffee-pots, teapots, sharp paring knives, and cleaning supplies.

The mixing center maybe a simple counter between two work areas.  It needs several electrical outlets.  Storage is needed for measuring, mixing, and baking equipment.  An electric mixer food processor, and blender may be stored here.  Storage space is needed for cake mixes, flour, sugar, and other baking ingredients.

You may want an eating center, which could be a counter with tables or chairs or a separate table and chairs.   Stools work at the high counter.  Remember with chairs to be pulled out, is there enough room to go behind Extra space could be used on the sides for traffic passageway.  If you have plenty counter space, you may choose to have a small appliance center.  Frequently used appliances, if small should be kept on the counter, If you can mount under the counter or on the wall any of your small appliances, you'll save counter work space.  A planning center may be part of the kitchen.  It would include a desk or chair at a counter area.  Put the computer here.  Use the computer to manage your food grocery shopping, which will turn into fully balanced menus.  Any recipes you don't know the computer will give you a copy.  The computer could also set up a chore list for all family members to help keep up with a clean democratic house.  Laundry may be in the kitchen with a hidden stacked washer and dryer.  Don't forget to keep the cookbooks, recipe files, and telephone, with all household records.  Actually the computer is the organizer or supervisor of your household finances and plans.  Software needs to be stored too.  Don't forget if  possible to set up your three major work centers-range-refrigerator/freezer- and sink.  The work triangle causes the most efficient work triangle  in a kitchen with the sink-----range----refrigerator/freezer.  All must be equally apart.  The equidistant amount of steps between the three points of the work center makes it the most efficient work center. Families must check and recheck to see that the new house they wish to buy or rent has the necessary work triangles. There will be less steps between an equal triangle instead of all three work areas are on a straight line where you walk from end to end to get to all the work centers.

## SKILL 23.2 Traffic Patterns, Room Arrangements, Storage Facilities, and Family Needs. Look for ways to Avoid Crossing any Traffic Pattern, Room Arrangements, Storage Facilities, and Family Needs.

Ideally all through traffic is people going through the new house. The three appliances should be in a triangular shape. Through traffic should be outside the triangle in the kitchen. Or it will cause confusion, congestion, , and accidents.

## SKILL 23.3 Home Energy Usage and Ways to Conserve Energy

Electricity is the major energy use in the home. Some families supplement their energy with sun panels on the roof that capture the solar energy that's converted to electricity, Others heat with gas. Gas prices keep going up. More and more homes are turning to total electricity in their homes cause gas is much more costly. One good idea for home energy efficiency is to contact the local utility department. They can go through your house and make suggestions how to conserve energy. Close your drapes when the bright sun is out on that side of the house. Be sure there's no leaks by doors or windows. Make your home air-tight. Put up fans. They help circulate the cold air. Cook on a grill during the summer. Keep the extra heat outside of the house. Try not to overheat your kitchen by cooking on the stove. Sit one evening and enjoy the evening candlelight. Again less electricity used. If you have a workable fireplace, use some logs to warm the house. On weekends try to cook up several dinners in duplicate. Put them labeled in the freezer. When you are hungry later during the week, simply microwave as much as you can eat.

## SKILL 23.4 Home Construction-Maintenance, Repairs, Aesthetics, and Family Needs.

When you decide to build your home, or at least work with a builder, you'll have a huge job. Find the property to build on and buy it. Now get the architect to help you set the floor plans. Include any extra crook and cranny you ever wanted. Include all your dreams. Have the large backyard landscaped with a tiny bridge by the pond. Think of aesthetics, the beauty of this home. There is the bridge and beautiful landscaping with trees. The pool has a corner that has five airjets to make a jaccuzzi. The pool area is screened in. The patio is furnished with lounges, chairs, tables, and cocktail tables. It's a comfortable place for a cookout. The kitchen has a huge eat in area and a large kitchen for food preparation. The most modern appliances are equipped in the kitchen. So super meals are prepared. There's a medium dinning room with a hand blown glass chandelier above the table. The dinning room isn't used except during family holiday get togethers. The living room is well furnished, yet seldom used. It's a leftover room needed when extra company comes over that can't fit in the den. The den or family room is the most comfortable room in the house. There's a sectional leather couch. Plenty of room to sit or recline. The entertainment center is in here. It includes the television, stereo, and several hand held video games. Lots of photographs are on the shelves with plants. There's three great art deco pictures on the walls as well as both boys have awards up. As the family increases, more room for toys, beds, etc. need to be set up. Sometimes families turn the garage into an extra room. As far as aesthetic are concerned, beauty is in the eye of the beholder. Maintenance and repairs are necessary at the time of the breakdown. Charge if you can't afford to fix the repair. Things need to work well to have a household in primo shape. If you leave repairs undone, your, property will soon look like Sanford and Son on television. Maintenance includes roof-pressure cleaning every few years to get rid of the mildew. You could clean with the pressure cleaning with one part bleach and 3 parts water. You can clean the driveway and sidewalks too. Paint every 5 years inside the house and about every 7 years till you have to repaint the outside of the house. Maintenance of any household appliance isn't cheap either. Maintenance and repairs at your own household isn't cheap when someone makes a house call. But they are your responsibility to keep working.

Remember aesthetics makes your residence your own domain as pretty as in HOUSE BEAUTIFUL. It is your castle. Take care of it!

## COMPETENCY 24.0 INTERIOR DESIGN                    2.1%

### SKILL 24.1 Housing Fashioned by Elements and Principles of Design

Principles of design men consider Harmony when the whole is achieved in a pleasing manner to the whole. Proportion-where size, length, and bulk relate to each other. Third is Balance-where there are two equal images at both ends from the center. Fourth is Rhythm-where the eye flows to all points of interest from the center. Fifth is Emphasis where you'll look to one image of the outfit or room and everything else falls in the background. Don't forget the components of color, texture, print,proportion. Line ,proportion, and balance, must be controlled in a fashion design. Just like line can add height to a room. If you wallpaper you can create illusions. You may like a border. The border at the top of the wall near the ceiling looks excellent. Or you may put the border half way from floor and ceiling. That's called a wainscot. Balance must be controlled. Color whether tinted or shaded sets the mood. There can be intensity or a mild colored room.. Hot colors like red or orange add to the size of this room. Cool colors like blue or green are relaxing to the psyche. Both the basic elements and principles of design control the interior space.

### SKILL 24.2 Wall, Window, and Floor Treatments

First consider your budget. How much can you afford? There are several floor possibilities. You could put down a wooden floor and use throw rugs. Carpeting has a range of costs as well as a range of many blends of carpets to choose from. Look for durability. You can put down linoleum, which is durable with light maintenance, and low cost. Many of the linoleums look like expensive tile. Tile is high costing, but it lasts forever. It needs too be swept and mopped.

For wall treatments try paint, wallpaper, add stucco. There are several paint styles. Just a plain color. Or you can sponge over the base color, or you can cover the base color with a feather brush. These two methods mane the walls look wallpapered. Painting is the lowest in cost. You can tile the walls also.

Window treatments are many. You can choose verticals with a valance. You could get horizontal shades. Balloon shades are soft looking and popular. Curtains or double rod curtains that just push open. You can try shutters and paint them. Try french pulled back drapes. They're quite elegant. Pull a shade down to keep the light and heat out of the room with the french drapes. The verticals you put up can be wallpapered to match the room wall treatments. Any of this that you can do on your own lower the window treatments costs.

## SKILL 24.3 Furniture, Traffic Patterns, and Focal Points

When you set up a room, say the living room, put the furniture on the walls. Make a conversation area and a television entertainment center. Heavier pieces need to be balanced with a few lighter pieces. Remember to have a certain path for traffic through the room. The focal point may be the etegers holding some trophies or family heirlooms. You may have a space for your computer and software. The traffic pattern should not break up a conversation area or television viewing either. If you like plants, put a six foot palm in one of the corners behind a swivel cloth chair. This makes for a super environmental focal point. Remember in all rooms that less is best. Put in the necessary basics like a bed or a couch or a table. Add slowly and carefully to the basics and add items that are acceptable accessaries.

## COMPETENCY 25.0   FURNITURE and EQUIPMENT                    2.1%

### SKILL 25.1  Design, Scale, Proportion, and Need

Any type of furniture style in a house should coordinate or blend.  For instance Queen Anne chairs are bulky and large.  They don't match up with country oak.  You can match formica furniture nicely with any Lucite piece.  Wicker can go with most other light furniture stays such as Lucite, rattan, and nicely with formica as well as leather.  Heavy furniture can't mix with large Roman or Grecian  huge pieces.  The furniture appears to take over the people and then the room.  There are  many rules of design.  Remember HARMONY-all goes together, PROPORTION-where size, length, and width relate.  BALANCE-it's equal on both sides.  RHYTHM-where the eyes flow from one point to the other.  EMPHASIS-where your eye goes directly  too all the rest is simply background.  Don't forget color, texture, print, or proportion.  Mix prints very seldom or you'll get a busy look.  With proportion, be sure all looks in balance throughout the room.  Textures seem to mix pretty nicely.  Scale means pieces mesh in size.  Family need is the reason to save for any furniture.  Let's say junior is in the oven.  With a baby more things will be needed.  The family must pull together so that the needs can be met.  Equipment necessary would be kitchen equipment, laundry facilities, and lawn mowing equipment. An air conditioner or refrigerator-freezer is extremely expensive if needed to be replaced.  Do you need a large new appliance?  How much space do you have?  Is it easy to clean?  Is the warranty good?  Do you need the extra features?  Where are the temperature controls?   Does the door open to the right or the left?  Which way must the door open in your kitchen.  What's the yearly energy costs?  Is it enough space?  Is it manual defrost, cycle defrost, or frost-free model?   Do you want an automatic ice maker, throuout the door from a dispenser, or glide out on rollers.  All extra accessories raise the price of the appliance.  You can invest in a freezer if you have room for  it.  If you buy a range consider a freestanding model, a built-in model, or a counter model.  Do you want a gas or electric range?  Do you want a self-cleaning or. continuous cleaning oven.  Do you want a pilotless ignition?  Do you want an induction cooktop?   A combination oven is pretty neat with a microwave and a conventional oven in one.  Or to you want to put your microwave above the conventional oven.  People   like dishwashers.  Most future kitchens will be equipped with computers.

### SKILL 25.2  Home Furnishings,Materials,Care,andWorkmanship

Home Furnishings do not Seem to be as well made as in the 1950's-1960's.  Most American Homes are well furnished from kitchen to living, to bedrooms.  In the earlier days there was a craftmanship in furniture construction. The materials used now seem cheaper than fifty years ago.  The needs  of the family are still the same.  We need shelter, clothing, food, and love.  In the shelter coordinate the furnishings and the accessaries.  Have  a colorscheme in every room.  Have one major hue for each room. Fill in with one or two recessive colors like make the den beige. Add color like green with plants and pillows. Add pillows to the couch and add another background color. No matter the accessaries, try to get the most for your money. The material available for home products must be thoroughly checked because there's a lot of inferior materials. If you can have more of an artist to make furniture or accessories for you, do it. This mass production looses something in craftsmanship. What ever you spend your money on, you want to take good care of it.

## COMPETENCY 27.0  MEAL PLANNING

### SKILL 27.1  Cultural, Socioeconomic, and Geographic Factors Influence Food Choices

When it comes to meal planning, first you need to check your resources. You need protein foods.  Remember nutrition at all times.  You need a variety of foods.  A culture is a group with beliefs, customs, and traditions shared.  They are passed down from generation to generation.  Geography effects food choices.  If by the sea, fish is a super source of protein.  Rice in the orient since it's moist in the soil.  Socioeconomic effects food choices just by what you are exposed to.  If in an upper class level you'll surely know what caviar and escargot are.  If you are in the lower class level,  meat will be rare in your household.  Hash would be a terrific meal.  Again you may be malnourished in any level of socioeconomics.  Whether poor, middle class, or upper class.  It's your food choices that matter.  I can understand how culture can influence your food choices.

If you feel the cow is sacred then you do not want to eat beef or veal. Moslems do not eat pork.  Many orthodox Jews don't eat pork either.  They keep Kosher and separate milk and meat products.  But the ones closest to a lake or the sea will have an abundance of fish to eat.  A natural geographic supplier of fish is the best resource of protein.

### SKILL 27.2  Asthetically Pleasing Meals

You need to use your resources to make this meal.  That is time, skill, food supply, money, and knowledge.  Think of what foods go good together.  This is meal management.  Be sure the meal you plan is nutritious.  Planning saves you time and energy.   Plan ahead, work efficiently,  and conserving natural resources.  Time to decorate food before serving is nice.  Be sure that what you serve looks, smells, and tastes good.  Foods must complement each other in flavor, texture, color, shape, size, and temperature.  Flavors should harmonize. Use only one strong-flavored food per meal.  Contrast textures will make the meal more interesting.  Mix up soft and mushy or hard and crisp in  one meal. Select foods in many colors in one meal.  Color stimulates the appetite.  Fruits and vegetables  add color to many meals. Try to use many shapes of  foods and sizes.  Examples would be to cube, dice, or slice the food.  Vary the food temperatures in each meal.  Read the recipe beforehand.  Do the necessary pre-preparation like chopping, marinating, or peeling an orange.  Don't forget to make the table look pretty.  Use a tablecloth and all matching dishes.  Set the table properly.  Try a flower centerpiece.   Use your table manners.

## SKILL 27.3 Budget and Management Factors to Plan, the Purchase, and Preparation of Food.

You should know by now to look on the food label to see that the food is Nutritious for the expiration date on the label to see how long the food will be ok to eat. The bar code or line code that is scanned at the register tells allot about the product including the cost. Learn to compare prices with UPC, Universal Product Code, that's the label or ticket by the product at the store on the edge of the shelf. UPC tells the price per unit like ounces or pounds. This way you can figure out the better buy when reading the UPC. Smart shopping can help you get the most nutrition for your money. Make a grocery list and stick to it. Plan your menus in advance. Remember nutrition is vital. Planning ahead is your meal management. If you have a home computer, you can keep a food inventory. When you are ready to shop, the computer can create your shopping list. Arrange your list in order of your grocery stores floor plan. Be flexible with the shopping list. Something may be a better buy because it's on sale this week. Cross off the list each item found on the shelf. Don't shop when you are hungry. Compare stores. Is one cleaner than another? Are there generic products that are cheaper? If so buy generic. Take advantage of coupons or refunds. If you do not need the item, don't use the coupon. Don't buy it.

## COMPETENCY 28.0 PRINCIPLES of FOOD SELECTION and STORAGE

### SKILL 28.1 Food Label System

There is a world of information on a food label. Read them to make better choices. The law, FDA, Food and Drug Administration, requires certain information on the label. The product name, net weight or net contents. The name and the address of the manufacturer, packer, or distributor are on the food label. The ingredients are listed in descending order. The label tells you exactly what you're getting. The label cannot be false or misleading. It may have a picture. If the food is imitation, it must list it perishable, those that spoil easily. There must be instructions for storing those foods. Directions to prepare the food should be there too. If a food is enriched or fortified it must have a nutrient label. It goes by serving size, servings per containers, and calories per serving. The following nutrients are listed : protein, carbohydrates, fat, vitamins A,C,B,D, and B6, calcium, iron, phosphorus, and magnesium.

### SKILL 28.2 Unit Pricing or Dating of Products

Unit pricing means figuring the cost per ounce or pound. It's usually on a tag attached to the shelf at the grocery store by food. Unit pricing lets you compare different size packages. Compare different forms of food. Peaches come fresh, frozen, canned, or dried. Compare the cost of convenience foods against the cost of ingredients for homemade. Plan your food choices around lower-priced foods. Open dating is a date stamped on a food package. There are four types of dates stamped on a food package. Pack date is when the food product was manufactured, processed, or packaged. Pull or sell date is the last day the product should be sold. Freshness date is on the product to tell when it is best to be used. The expiration date is the last date the product should be used.

### SKILL 28.3 Government Grades and Policies as Set by the U.S. Department of Agriculture (USDA) the Food and Drug Administration (FDA), and Other Recognized Agencies

Milk must be Grade A pasteurized to be shipped between states for retail sale. FDA sets up the standards for the highest quality. Butter is graded by USDA as AA,A, or B. Grade B butter is made from sour cream. Some cheeses are graded by the USDA. Grade AA is the finest quality cheese. Grade A is good. The USDA inspects poultry. Grade A is the highest. There is grade B for poultry. Eggs are sold by grade and size. The grade is shown on the sheild on the egg carton. Grade AA is the highest for eggs. Grade A eggs are good for poaching or frying. Grade B eggs are fine for baking. USDA grade beef, veal, and lamb are prime, choice, and good. Prime is the top grade with marbling. Choice is a high quality that you can buy it in the grocery store. Good grade is lower in cost. Pork is not graded although the USDA inspects it.

**HOME ECONOMICS**

## SKILL 28.4  Product Standards

Some foods do not have to list the ingredients because they are on the FDA Standard of Identity List. Foods like jelly or ketchup are on the list. Thus they need not list their ingredients on the label. The government keep a close eye on most products found in the supermarket. There are consumer advocates like Ralph Nader that report bad or deceiving products.

## SKILL 28.5  Effects of Heating, Cooling, Dehydrating, and Crystallizing of Food Quality

Sometime when heating foods the taste gets better. Think of eating raw roast beef. Cooking makes the meat edible. Yet heating some foods ruin them. Ice cream would melt. Ice cream must be frozen. Cooling foods is a must just after serving. Don't leave food sitting on the counter. Wrap foods tightly, label, and put in the refrigerator. Cakes are cooled on the wire rack along with cookies. There are different ways to heat food. You can microwave, bake in the oven, heat on top of the oven, or grill. You cool the food in the freezer or the refrigerator. I make food last much longer. The temperature is below zero Centigrade or below 32 degrees Fahrenheit. The low temperature will protect the foods from spoilage. Dehydration is an interesting process on food. All of the moisture is removed from the food either sun dried or microwaved. You can buy a small appliance called a dehydrater. This process works well with fruits. They get a raisin texture. Crystallization is cooking a liquid to a solid form. Peanut brittle or rock candy are crystallized. All the processes mentioned are fine for food quality. The processes make the food change form.

## SKILL 28.6  Food Additives

Food additives are used to preserve food. This makes it last longer. Sometimes the additives enhance the appearance, flavor, or texture of the recipe. Many additives prevent food spoilage, add nutrients, give color, or flavor. They can be a natural substance or a manufactured one. Salt and Indian spices for flavor or preservation were the first food additives. Without additives our food supply would be seriously limited. Several additives are stabilizers. Additives add nutrients, give flavor, preservation, keep texture smooth, chewy, or crunchy. Emulsifiers keep an oil mixture well blended like in mayonnaise. Artificial coloring can be added to a food to keep it looking appetizing. Additives control acidity. They help age foods like cheese. Foods that say enriched or fortified simply mean that nutrients are added. The FAD regulates foods shipped interstate and the government consumer safety offices inspect where foods are processed. The Food Safety and Inspection Service (FSIS) of the USDA also watches the manufacturers to make sure the food is safe. GRAS list also is a government list of approved food additives. Stricter food additive laws were passed in 1958. Sugar, salt, and spices on the GRAS list are approved as safe by the government.

## SKILL 28.7  Quality of Food Products-Preparation, Storage, and Preservation.

Careful preparation of food is a must. You need the proper tools. Buy only tools you will use. Get good construction tools. Think of tool storage at home. Always store tools closest to the place of use. Storage is necessary. For preparation it's convenient to use your appliances. Use a portable electric appliance whenever possible. Check the warranty, name and address of company guaranteeing. Exactly who, what, and how long is coverage usable. Food processor is terrific for meal preparation for grating, chopping, slicing, and to mix ingredients. Look for the UL seal. It says it's been tested and is a super buy. Toaster, oven, mixer, electric skillet, blender, slow cooker, coffee maker are your best buys. Then there's the major appliances. Storage space can be added with a pegboard on the wall to hold pots and pans, and cooking utensils. Now you can use a cabinet for foods as a pantry. Just keep cold foods cold and hot foods hot to avoid spoilage.

Then store correctly and well packaged. Preservation in any food product makes it last longer. It adds hundreds of foods to the supermarket. All three proper preparation, storage, and preservation give us a variety of foods in an abundant supply in the U.S. physiological effects of food additives isn't really bad. If you have reactions to these specific foods as harmful to you, stop eating them right away. Preparation must be perfect. Follow the recipe. Storage must be perfect, and preservation increases the food supply with the use of additives. Preservatives cause food to last longer. Without proper storage for that food it will spoil. Preservation once again will save many convenience foods. TV trays, frozen dinners last in the freezer for an entire year. Some frozen foods can be all a person eats, they must store them the right way. If a food has no preservatives it will spoil easily. Preservation keeps foods a stronger food product.

## COMPETENCY 29.0    FOOD PREPARATION KNOWLEDGE.          4.1%

### SKILL 29.1   Food Safety with Local and State Agencies.

To keep food safe you need to have clean personal hygiene. Otherwise you can transfer bacteria to the food when handselling it. Wash your hands if you cough, sneeze, go to the bathroom, play with your pets, touch raw meat, wear clean clothes and an apron. Roll up long sleeves. Tie back long hair. Keeping the kitchen clean is just as important as using fresh foods. Insects and rodents carry harmful bacteria. They must be removed by you or an exterminator immediately. If you make sure there aren't crumbs around or spills, you should be aright. Take the garbage out daily. If you can any foods examine the jars closely for mold, bubbling, spurting liquid, strange odor, or cloudiness. Any of these signs show food spoilage or food poisoning. Be careful to discard right away. Foods that are to be stored dry in a pantry or cabinet are breads, crackers, beans, sweetener, seasoning, and dry mixes. Again cold foods go in the refrigerator. Frozen foods should be labeled and dated for storage in the freezer. Rotate freezer foods so that the oldest is used first . Be sure foods for the freezer are air tight, wrapped very well.

It is the FDA that decides which substances are legal to foods. The first additives were salt and sugar. The FDA's job is to establish safe levels of chemical use in foods by research and experiments. Before stricter food additives laws were passed in 1958, 700 additives were already in use. These approved ingredients were classified on the GRAS list. Often times you get sick with the flu, when actually it was a food-borne illness like food poisoning. Sometimes there isn't an odor or off-flavor. Some toxins are not even, killed by heat. Some bacteria produce spores. The local and state agencies check food plants and slaughter houses to be sure they are sanitary. They check the stores that sell the food too. If any thing is not up to code, the owner of the restaurant will be fined .

### SKILL 29.2  Safety and Sanitary Procedures in the Production, Processing, Handleling, and Food Storage.

When procssing foods like canning, be very careful not to contaminate the food. Do this by keeping you self clean. Keep the kitchen clean. Keep the foods at the right temperature. Hot foods should be hot and cold foods cold, You need to avoid food-borne illness like salmonellosis perfringen poisoning, staphyylococcal poisoning, and botulism. Bacteria are normally in food. Most of it comes from careless food handeling. So for sanitation just keep that kitchen food; and yourself clean. Pets must not be in the kitchen while you cook. Get rid of bugs with Raid or an extrerminator. Some foods must be kept at 40F in a refrigerator. If left out too long it will get bacteria on the food. This could be very dangerous. Wear clean clothes and a clean apron. Roll up long sleeves. Tie long hair back. If you cough or sneeze, wash your hands, right away. Empty the kitchen trash every day.

Before cooking wash the counter tops and tables. Be certain that cookware and kitchen tools are clean. Wipe up spills as you work. If raw meat is placed on the counter, wipe it up with soapy hot water. Plastic cutting boards that are poisonous. Becareful how long you freeze or refrigerate food. Look for the pull date on many products. Don't use them after that date, at a picnic only allow food out on the table for one hour no longer. Just watch your temperatures. Hot foods hot and cold foods cold.

## SKILL 29.3  Food-borne Illness

Food contaminated with harmful bacteria does not always have an off-flavor or an odor. Sometimes the toxins are not even killed when heated. Spores grow on spoiled food. When one eats bad food the symptoms like the flu may appear 3-12 hours later after eating depending on the type of bacteria. Common food-borne illness are salmonellosis, perfringen, staphloccocal poisoning, and botulism. Bacteria are naturally present in food when you buy it. Salmonella can be found in raw meat, poultry, eggs, and dairy products. Sanitation means keeping food at the proper temperature. Don't forget proper food handeling. Keep the food at the proper temperatures. Keep yourself clean. Keep the kitchen clean. Keep the food at proper temperatures.

Salmonellosis is carried by insects, rodents, and pets like turtles, birds, dogs, and cats. The bacteria grows and multiplies at 60'F up to 125'F. Symptoms would be a headache, vomiting, diarrhea, stomach cramps, and fever. Severe infections cause high fever and even death. Prevention is done by washing raw foods. Keep hot foods hot, above 140'F to destroy bacteria. Keep hands, counters, and clean utensils. This helps stop the spread and growth of salmonella.

Prefringens poisoning is caused by eating food contaminated with large amounts of bacteria. This happens when there are a large group being fed, like a community dinner. This is a spore-forming bacteria grown without oxygen. Spores are everywhere in food, soil, dust, and sewage. High temperatures kill bacteria but not spores. Symptoms are nausea, diarrhea, and inflamed intestine. Prevention is to serve cooked food right away at 140'F. Serve cold foods right away or keep at 40'F until being served.

Staphylococcal poisoning is caused by eating food containing the toxin. It's transmitted by food handlers who carry the bacteria. This bacteria is resistant to heat. · This bacteria grows between 60'Fand125'F. Symptoms are vomiting, diarrhea, tired, and stomach cramps. The bacteria doesn't grow below 40'F or above 140'F. Cleanliness prevents the spread of bacteria.

Botulism caused by eating food with the toxin. Found in soil and water. Symptoms are doublevision, inability to swallow, 65% of people in the United States die from this. Again never eat or taste from a can that is bulging, damaged, or leaking. Never eat food that does not smell normal. When in doubt throw it out.

To eliminate the chances of food-borne illness, keep a clean kitchen. Scrub your hands if you sneeze, cough, go to the bathroom, play with pets, or touch raw foods. Be sure your clothes are clean, roll up long sleeves, tie back long hair, wash hands after a cough or a sneeze. Keep the kitchen spotlessly clean. No pets, wash the counters, pots and pans, and dirty dishes. Wipe up spills immediately. Sweep the floor. Use clean dishcloths and dishtowels. Be sure to wrap foods airtight to store properly. Label and date the food for the freezer. The rule is keep hot foods hot and cold foods cold. Bacteria must have a food to grow on, with moisture, and the right temperature to grow.

### SKILL 29. 4 Selection, Use, and Care of Kitchen Equipment

The refrigerator holds highly perishable foods. When buying kitchen appliances, remember a few points. Stay within your budget. Know the amount of space it will fit in at your house. Check the energy label. Don't buy accessories that you do not need, like water or ice served outside the freezer door. Is the refrigerator frost-free or cycle defrost. It will cost less if the freezer is manually defrosted, but you may not want to deal with this chore. Not only the large appliances take thought a c comparison shopping at several stores, so do the smaller kitchen equipment. Electrical appliances that make a task easier are usually expensive. With all that you'll want and need for the kitchen, buy a few new pieces weekly or monthly. Whatever your budget allows.

Start with dry measuring cups. Liquid measuring cups are needed next. One measures volume the other measures net weight. You need measuring spoons and a scoop to mix up dry ingredients. Use a straight edge spatula to level off dry ingredients or for spreading frosting on a cake. You need a good set of cutting tools. Get a paring knife to pare fruits and vegetables. The utility knife is an all around knife. The chef's knife sometimes called a French knife. It's a large rectangular blade. A butcher's knife cuts apart meats. The bread knife has a serrated edge. The boning knife cuts up poultry. A slicing knife is long and narrow for cutting meat. The carving knife is for slicing meats. The kitchen shears cut apart fruits and vegetables. A sharpening steel is used to sharpen the edge of a knife. The peeler takes off the outer edge of fruits and vegetables. A cutting board to protect the counter when cutting is a must. Buy a plastic, not wooden cutting board. The wooden boards get cracks where germs can hide and contaminate your meat. Get a grater to shred cheese.

Starting out in your own household, you'll need mixing tools. There are electric mixers, but all these steps can be done by hand to make a cake. Start out with mixing bowls. Glass pottery, metals, or plastic bowls as a set are perfect. Use a rubber scraper to remove food stuck on the sides of a bowl. Use a rotary beater too mix ingredients like for pancake batter. A wire whisk beats and blends like with sauces. A flour sifter adds air to flour and other dry ingredients.

Baking tools needed when starting out are a pastry blender, rolling pin, pastry board with a cloth, cookie cutters, and a pastry brush.

Now you need cooking tools. A wooden spoon to mix hot foods. A basting spoon to put liquid over a roasting meat. A slotted spoon removes liquid from foods. Tongs turn hot foods. The baster looks like a big eye dropper. It's used to put liquid on the meat while it cooks to keep it moist. A ladle serves soup or punch. A turner flips over a food. A potato masher to make mashed potatoes. Kitchen forks have two times to lift foods.

Then there are kitchen aids to the equipment like a can opener, bottle opener, a timer, thermometers, strainers, a colander, and a vegetable brush. A food grinder to grind meat like liver for chopped liver. The grinder is used to make your hamburger at the grocery store. Have good pot holders or oven mitts near the stove to lift hot pans. A funnel comes in handy to fill small-mouthed containers. Wire cooling racks help cool cookies, cakes, and breads.

Cookware is needed for on top of the stove and in the oven. There are many types of material used to make pots, and pans. It pays to spend more because you want your cookware to last as long as a marriage. I have my wedding gifts of faberware for twenty years and it still looks like new. Get frying pans and skillets, usually around ten inches in diameter. Lids help when grease splatters. Sauce pans and pots with lids come in a variety of sizes. Get if you can afford it, a one quart, two quart, and three quart pans. You may want a double boiler to heat things that burn easily like chocolate or sauces. You may want a pressure cooker. Here the food is cooked under pressure in steam, which reduces the cooking time. You may like a griddle to put over a stove burner and make pancakes, toast, eggs, or grilled sandwich. You must have an oven roasting pan with a rack. This is good for large meats. A soup kettle makes soup and corn on the cob. A steamer is super to steam vegetables. You need an area for planning shoppinglists and keeping records. You may have cookbooks and cake pan shapes. You need a pie pan and a cookie sheet. A loaf pan for meatloaf or bread. A muffin tin for cupcakes, rolls, or muffins. A jelly-roll pan for cookies and a tube pan for cakes.

You need to have storage room for all this kitchen equipment. Don't let it just sit in the cabinet. Get out your things and create beautiful, edible projects in the kitchen. Care means keeping it clean, use SOS pads for stuck on food. If the handle is loose, tighten it up, use a screwdriver. You can purchase your kitchen equipment and utensils. You can buy your needed kitchen items at any department store in the housewares department. If necessary go to the Goodwill or Faith Farm. You'll find used kitchen equipment there at a lower cost, yet in perfect condition. Go to garage sales too.

### SKILL 29.5 Organization and Management in Arrangement and Use of Kitchen Facilities and Equipment.

Some houses use the kitchen for several reasons, like a child play area too, or there's a small office in the kitchen corner. There are specific work areas as in any kitchen. We call them work centers, like the mixing or cooking area. The utensils are always stored closest to the place of use. There are four major work centers in the kitchen.

The refrigerator -freezer center needs counter space. Then there is the range center. It is the focal point in the kitchen. The microwave is in this area too. The range area also needs counter space. There is need for a cabinet or near by pantry for food. The cooking utensils, pots, and pans in storage belong to this center. Then there is the sink or cleanup center by the sink with a dishwasher, food disposal, and if possible a trash compacter. Cleanup includes washing dishes, cleaning fruits, and other foods. Next is the mixing center with plenty of counter space. It requires electrical outlets. Storage is needed for baking equipment, like a mixer, food processor, and a blender storage space in a pantry or cabinet is needed for cake mixes, flour, sugar, and other baking ingredients. Other centers may be included like an eating area or counter with tools. You may want a sit down desk in the kitchen for planning menus, making shopping lists, and keeping record. You may have cookbooks here and a calendar. If you're lucky, you'll have a computer too.

Never forget the work triangle. That is between the range-refrigerator-freezer and the sink. The work flow is how you move around in the work triangle. It is ideal when the three major points of the triangle are equal distance apart like an equalateral triangle. You don't want people to walk through your work triangle. That traffic pattern needs to be eleminated.

There are different kitchen plans. There are five common ones. They are a one-walled corridor, L-shaped, U-shaped, and island kitchens.

Check that the kitchen is big enough for you and with plenty of storage space. Is there good lighting? Does the kitchen have an exhaust system to rid heat, odors, and steam. Is there plenty of storage? Are there enough electrical outlets? Be sure the kitchen area is sanitary, moisture-proof, and heatproof. Be sure there's enough lighting. Ground the appliances. Floors must be durable and easily wiped up. Wall coverings should be washable. You shouldn't forget to decorate. Add color. Use an attractive spice rack. Plants look nice in a kitchen.

Kitchen equipment and appliances are costly. All the cookware you purchase should be used. Don't buy a full set and let some pots and pans never to be used. Buy durable and solid construction. Check the balance of the utensil. Are the handles easy to grasp. Lids should fit securely. Is it easy to lift? Know your budget and stay within it. Check the energy guide labels on the appliances. Check for warranties.

For small equipment that are portable you can save time. Check on a toaster, mixer, electric skillet, blender, slow cooker, and coffee maker.

Major appliances are refrigerator-freezer, freezer, range, and a microwave oven. You may want a dishwasher too. You can even purchase used appliances. Be sure they work and have a warranty for a while.

## SKILL 29.6  Food Preparation Techniques

A recipe tells you the ingredients and instructions for preparing a specific food. Be sure the recipe includes a complete list of ingredients in order of use. Then look for specific instructions that are step by step. Is the pan size listed? What is the yield? Recipes are in one of three styles. That's the standard form. with ingredients listed first and the directions follow. There's the action form where the ingredients are listed beside the directions. The narrative form lists the ingredients and directions in a paragraph. Sometimes you may be out of an ingredient and can sustitute another one. If you want to increase or decrease recipes, be careful not to change the basic recipe.

You must measure accurately. Use standard measuring cups and spoons. When measuring dry ingredients level off the top with a spatula. If measuring liquids, put the measuring cup on the counter and check at eye level. To measure fats and oils check at eye level or use the water displacement method. Here you put liquid in the measuring cup. Add the solid shortening until the water raises up the amount of shortening you need. Most butter and margarine are labeled as tablespoons up to eight on the package. There are many techniques to use in the kitchen. I'll name a few you'll probably use often. To bake, saute, blend, chop, cube, dot, flake, grate, grease, knead, mince, peel, reduce, score, sift, stir, toss, or whip are all common food techniques.

There are basic cooking methods in liquid. They are boiling, simmering, poaching, or stewing. The cooking methods in moist heat include braising, steaming, or cooking in a plastic cooking bag. You can cook in fat if you're not watching your weight with panbroiling, panfrying, and sauteing, stir-frying, or deep-fat frying. If you cook with dry heat use baking, roasting, and broiling.

## SKILL 29.7  Finished Food Products and Characteristic Variations.

Different pan sizes effect baking products heighth and texture. Oven temperature too high the food won't rise and will burn. Too low of a temperature will dry out the food. Pies need to be baked at 425-450"F for twenty minutes. If the crust is brown, it's time to fill the pie. Fruits cooked in liquids breaks down the fiber, thus the form changes with heat. You can bake fruits or broil them. Broiiling fruits browns them. Fruits can be fried. Fruits can be sauteed until brown. You can microwave fruits. Be sure to cover the fruit for the microwave. Also vegetables can be made many ways which changes the characteristics of the food. Vegetables can be served raw and crunchy. If you cook these vegetables, the fiber is broken down and it's easier to chew. The flavor gets milder. If the vegetables are overcooked they get mushy. Vegetables can be cooked in liquids,steamed,baked,fried,stir-fried,creamed,scalloped, or glazed. To cook vegetables in water bring the water to a boil, then, add the vegetables. Cover the pan, bring, to a second boil. Now turn burner temperature down and simmer until vegetables are tender. Green, yellow, white, and red vegetables can be cooked nicely in a liquid. Steaming is another good technique to use on vegetables. Steam until tender, not mushy. Some vegetables are best baked in the oven like potatoes. Some vegetables are delicious if deep-fat fried. Stir-frying is when the vegetable is thinly sliced. Then cooked in a small amount of hot oil in a wok.

Some vegetables come alive with a sauce, like cheese melted on broccoli. Scalloped vegetables are cooked in a sauce in a casserole in an oven. Glazed vegetables like carrots or sweet potatoes. Try to add that extra touch to your foods. Follow directions on the food label. for preparation. If it says heat on stove or use a pressure cooker do so. The microwave oven is a quick way to heat up vegetables too.

Cooking meat affects it in several ways. It tenderizes it. It improves the texture and appearance. During cooking the meat becomes tender and juicy. Don't overcook or the meat will be tough and hard. Overcooked meat is hard to digest. Tender cuts of meats are cooked by dry heat, which is roasted, broiled, pan-broiled, or panfried. Less tender cuts must be cooked in liquid or moist heat. Slow cooking less tender cuts need to be cooked in liquid for a longer period of time. Some techniques help tenderize the meat prior to cooking. You can grind, pound, or cut the meat to break down the connective tissues. Acids like a marinade to help break up the connective tissues of the meat. If the cut of meat is tender you can cook it with dry or moist heat. If a lower temperature is used during cooking ,the meat will be less tough. You can purchase a thermometer to stick inn the cut of meat, while cooking. This way you won't let the meat dry out and get tough.

Degree of doneness-rare, medium, or well done. Check with a small slit with a knife to see the interior of the meat. Then you'll be sure to get the cut cooked to your liking. Meat can be broiled, roasted, or pan-broiled. Meat can be fried in a pan or a deep fat fryer. Braising is popular for legs tender cuts of meat. Meat can even be microwaved.

Poultry can be prepared many ways. It may have to be boned first. See the recipe. Poultry must be cooked at moderate or low temperatures to be well done. Poultry can be cooked by broiling, roasting, frying, braising, and cooking in liquid. You can put poultry in the microwave oven too.

Fish can be cooked by dry-heat methods-broiling, baking, and panfrying. Never over cook. Fish can be braised, steamed, or poached.

Eggs can be scrambled, shirred, poached, and even microwaved.

When pasta is cooked, boil water in a large pot. Put the noodles in for 10-12 minutes. Rice is also cooked in liquid. Follow directions on the package. Don't use the microwave oven for rice or pasta,. There's no time saved there. Fats and oils make baked products tender. They add the richness to the crust of a pie. Eggs have many purposes in baking. They keep batters from separating when beaten.

Liquids help flour form the structure of baked products. Yeast breads have smoother texture than quick breads. Of course, the difference is the leavening agent. Quick breads are like pancakes or Christmas fruit cake. Yeast breads take more time to prepare. You knead the dough and let it rise. There are five different types of cookies. Depending on the method of preparation, the cookie could be crispy or moist and chewy. Ingredient amounts makes the difference.

Types of cookies are bar, like brownie, drop like chocolate chips, molded like Mexican wedding cakes, pressed are like spritz cookies. Rolled are hardened dough like Christmas shaped cookies. Refrigerator are shaped like a log and hardened in the refrigerator for several hours. They can be sliced or made into pinwheels. Cakes are shortened if fat goes into it. It is then more tender. Foam cakes have no fat. they are leavened by egg whites. They rise higher than shortened cakes. They are much lighter. Pies can be served with a top crust or not. Some have meringue for the top. It's easy to make soup from scratch. Basically all ingredients go into a large dutch oven and simmer.

## COMPETENCY 30.0 KNOWLEDGE OF FOOD SERVICE 4.1%

### SKILL 30.1 Table Setting and Table Service

Tableware is dinnerware, glasses, and flatware (silverware). One person placesetting is called a cover, with a dinner plate, salad plate, cup and saucer, an all-purpose bowl.

Dinnerware comes in china, earthenware, and stoneware, and plastic. Have a matching set. Glassware is in two shapes, tumblers or stemware. Flatware includes knives, forks, spoons, and serving pieces. To make a pretty table use table linens, like tablecloths, runners, placemats, and napkins. Make a special atmosphere to eat in. Put a flower center piece on the table or try candles.

Table service is how to serve those at the table their food. A buffet is the easiest with a large crowd. Have a serving counter. The guests can take what they want. The plate goes in the center. Knives on the right of the plate with the blade in towards the plate. Spoons are on the right of the knives. Forks stay to the left of the plate. Water glasses go above the knives. Coffee cup and saucer to the right of the spoons. The salad plate can be placed to the left of the fork. Napkin goes to the left of the forks.

Family style is informal. Food is put in serving dishes in the kitchen and then brought to the table. People pass around the serving dishes. Family style is good for everyday meals at home. Plate service is portioned out food on the plate. Restaurants use this service. Modified English service. Food is in serving pieces, yet the host or hostess dishes out your portions on your plate and passes it to you. Formal service is the most fancy style. The table is set with the fine silver, glassware, and a service plate. Plates are removed once used and given a new one. Compromise Service combines formal and English styles. Don't forget your table manners. Use your napkin. Don't talk with a mouth full.

## COMPETENCY 31.0 CURRICULUM DEVELOPMENT 3.1%

### SKILL 31.1 Home Economics Educators Professional Beliefs.

The blueprint for professional success is to prepare students for the workplace in the twenty-first century. The courses include developing human resources, work ethics, decision making skills, balancing work and the family, as well as other skills necessary to succeed in the work place that are not job-specific. Exploration of a variety of careers is recommended through a job shadowing experience. Courses still recommended at the high school level are child care provider, garment making, consumer technology in the home, food production and food sciences, home furnishings, life management skills, nutrition, parenting, clothing, and food production.

Home economics teachers feel that students learn living skills in our department. Here they prepare for life outside of high school. It's up to you to get prepared for the future.

### SKILL 31.2 Jobs in Family and Consumer Sciences

In the area of foods you can follow the career ladder. You start out as a kitchen helper, move up to sandwich maker, up to assistant cook, up to cook, up to assistant chef, up to executive chef. Careers in food and nutrition include those in food technology, food service, and in family consumer sciences. Food technologists help with engineering new products or packaging, or processing. This work helps improve flavor, appearance, and nutritional quality of processed foods. This insures a good food supply, work safety, sanitation, and quality control. Technologists handle world food problems. There are many jobs in the food service industry. That is the world of restaurants. In the restaurant there are many different jobs. In management there are owners, managers, executive chefs, dieticians, and assistant managers. These are the people that plan and supervise other workers. You may get jobs in education like being a Family and Consumer Sciences teacher. You can be a dietician at a hospital. You can get a job with any branch of the government to help feed the poor. Extension Service conducts educational workshops. Business uses Home Economists as spokes people or to write directions for use of the product; like a dishwasher.

You may work in the child care industry with proper supervision at all day cares. Or you might try to work in the fashion industry. Do you want to design or sew clothing?

### SKILL 31.3 Prevocational, Consumer Homemaking, and Job-preparation.

There are child care programs at several high schools. Here students learn to be preschool teachers. There are many jobs in the food industry. Take the basic foods classes at your local high school. Then sign up for the cooperative Foods service program during your junior and senior years. This way you work and get school credit plus cash. You get out of school early to go to work. You learn many leadership techniques in the CFS program.

## SKILL 31.4 National and Florida Trends That Affect Content Area.

It's a shame to admit but schools across the United States are dropping Home Economic classes. At least in California and various other states there's no living classes. This is a poor trend. I believe the practical skills taught in the family and consumer sciences department are necessary. Young people get out into the world without a clue what to do. In Life Management Skills students learn how to write checks, get a job, write a resume, where to look for a house or an apartment, how to shop, how to cook, how to eat right and so much more. It is a very useful course. Florida has kept Home Economics courses offered in middle and high schools. But Florida changed the name of Home Economics to Family and Consumer Sciences in 1996. Florida schools are far behind other states in education and slow to change. Florida schools are praised for keeping Home Economics courses in the schools. But the home economics content is learning to keep courses that lead students to a wage earning job like in the child care program or the Food service on the job training course.

## SKILL 31.5 National and Florida Legislation Has Affected the Historical Development of Home Economics.

Well interesting enough the name of Home Economics has been changed in many states. Florida changed Home Economics to Family and Consumer Sciences. Other states have changed the name too. But many states have iliminated home economics completely. Traditionally only women took home economics in high school. These women usually were planning to marry after high school and not attend college. Then in the 70's men started too sign up for Home Economics classes in high school. There was one class called Bachelor Survival. This was a semester course that covered cooking, basic sewing skills, child care, marriage and the family, and home management techniques.

Now in the '90's both sexes sign up for a variety of classes. Yes, the trend is to get rid of Home Economics in high schools. I hope that never happens because this is the only department that teaches directly living skills. Topics are covered here that must be addressed by our young. Topics like Marriage and the Family, Child Development, Banking and Money Management, Career Awareness, Foods and Cooking, Clothing Construction and fashions, Technology Preparation, and a Home Management, Aids, Suicide, and Teen Pregnancy.

**SKILL 31.6   International Events Affect our Families.**

When there is a war  in another country, it affects the  families of the  United States too.  That countries  resources are not on the international market.  If it's a country with oil and they are at war, we can't get any oil.  If we are in a war like dessert Storm, many United States men and women  will become soldiers and leave our land to defend it.  During World War II the United States  women ran the factories making weapons.  This change in the work force changed the family.  Dad goes off to war.  Mom now works eight hours a day at the factory. A baby-sitter watches the children if grandma isn't available.  But after the war ends, the men come home from war.  They want the job in the factories.  But the women liked the working and the money earning.  In the late 60's early 70's the competition between the sexes for the same job began.  By the 80's having two parents working became the norm.  Now kids go to after school day care.  The family has changed again.  There's less  quality time shared at home by the whole family.  During   the 90's the family began to fall apart.  There are 50% divorces out of all marriages.  There are different set ups for families now too. Like two families share  one house due to cost.  Or two women live together after divorce with their children.  Less and less are there nuclear families, of mom, dad, and the children.

**SKILL 31.7  Identify Student Organizations and National Agencies Related
             to Home Economics Education.**

The number one youth club in the United States according to Red Book Magazine is Future  Homemakers of America.  That's the club students in grades 6-12 and in a Home Economics class can join.   There are eight purposes promoting family-church-school.  There's the HERO club which stands for Home Economics Related Occupations.   If students are in the on the job training programs  like  CFS-Cooperative Food Service is a club.

Cooperative Extension Service most cities promotes Home Economics.  They hold workshops for the community  on things like  food safety.  There's Home Economics Association in most cities.  People with degrees in Home Economics can join.  There's a national Home Economics association.  There are Vocational Association to join too.

## COMPETENCY 32.0  PURPOSES and FUNCTIONS OF HOME ECONOMICS PROFESSIONAL ORGANIZATION.

### SKILL 32.1  Home Economics Associations

Basically, as mentioned above, the Home Economics Professional Organizations work to help the families in the community. The professionals get together for informative meetings. They give their time as volunteers at local homeless shelters. They serve on Holidays meals at the soup kitchen, food for the homeless. There's the American Home Economics Association. Then there are local Home Economics associations. Home Economists join together from education, business, food service, and the fashion scene.

### SKILL 32.2  Journals and Publications of Home Economics Professional Organizations.

There's the American Vocational Association Journal, Action, the American Home Economics Association, The Journal of Family and Consumer Sciences, and the American Vocational Journal to name a few of the publications for Home Economists.

## GOOD LUCK ON YOUR TEST!

## BIBLIOGRAPHY

Study from the following BIBLIOGRAPHY. competencies . The Department of Education feels these books will help prepare you for the certification exam.

1.American Red Cross. (1988). American Red Cross community CPR. Washington,DC:Author

2.Bee,H.(1989)The Developing Child(5th ed.).New York: Harper & Row

3.Clemens, A. (1957) Marriage and the Family. Englewood Cliffs,N.J. Prentice Hall.

4.Florida Department of Education, (1989). Vocational education program course standards: Home Economics education. Tallahassee, Fl:Author.

5.Helms,D. and Turner, J.(1986)Exploring Child Behavior (3rd edition). Belmont,California.

6.Iowa Home Economics Association. (1977) Unit method of clothing construction: Women's and men's wear (6th ed.) Ames,IA: Iowa State University Press.

7.Knox, D. (1988.) Choices in relationships: An introduction to marriage and the family(2nd ed.) St. Paul, MN: West.

8.Kowtaluk and Kopan.(1986). Food for Today. (3rd ed.) Peoria, Illinois.

9.Lowenthal,M.Thurber,M.,Chiriboga, D., and Associates.(1975)(1st ed.)San Francisco, California. Jossey-Bass, Inc.

10.Newberry and Fisher.(1986) The Food Book.Illinois. The Goodheart Wilcox Co.,Inc.

11.Nuttall,E.V.,Romero,I., Kalesnik,J.(1992) Assessing and Screening Preschoolers Psychological and Educational Dimensions .Needham, Mass. Simon and Schuster, Inc.

12Perry, Patricia (1973) The Vogue Sewing Book (2nd ed.) New York, New York, Butterick of American Can Co. Inc.

13Random House Book(1968) McCall's Sewing Book. New York, Random House, Inc.

14Wesley,F. and Sullivan,E.(1986)(2nd ed.)Human Growth and Development. New York, New York.

15Williams,S., & Worthington-Roberts,B. (eds.) (1993) Nutrition in Pregnancy and . St. Louis: Times Mirror/Mosby.

**Directions: Read each item and select the best response.**

1. **What is a calorie?**

   A. A way of measuring body fat by pinching the vein

   B. A fatty substance in foods that causes weight gain

   C. A unit that measures the heat energy of foods

   D. A substance similar to an amino acid

2. **Braising is a popular way of cooking:**

   A. Tender cuts of meat

   B. All cuts of meat

   C. Less tender cuts of meat

   D. Rib roast

3. **When you cut food into very small pieces, you are:**

   A. Paring

   B. Mincing

   C. Scoring

   D. Dredging

4. **Which nutrients are essential for the human body to function well?**

   A. Carbohydrates

   B. Proteins and fats

   C. Vitamins and minerals

   D. All of the above

5. **The nutrition label must list all these items EXCEPT:**

   A. Cholesterol per serving

   B. Serving size

   C. Number of servings

   D. Calories per serving

6. **Mutton is from:**

   A. Older sheep

   B. Young sheep

   C. Young cattle

   D. Older pigs

7. **People with heart disease may have to decrease their consumption of:**

   A. Complex carbohydrates

   B. Sodium and foods high in saturated fats

   C. Vitamins

   D. Proteins

8. **If adults do not eat less than they ate as adolescents:**

   A. Their weight will stay the same

   B. They will gain weight

   C. They will lose weight

   D. Their weight will depend on body type

9. **When buying a gas range, you should look for the:**

   A. UL seal

   B. FTC seal

   C. Energy Guide label

   D. AGA seal

10. **The cooking method you choose depends on all of the following EXCEPT:**

    A. Your personal preference

    B. The food you are preparing

    C. The equipment and the time available

    D. How many work centers are available

11. **What must the body have in order to carry on all the life processes?**

    A. Oxygen and water

    B. Variety of nutritious food

    C. Exercise and sleep

    D. All of the above

12. **Cooking tools should be stored in the:**

    A. Sink center

    B. Range center

    C. Mixing center

    D. None of these

13. A device that keeps too much electricity from flowing through the wires in an electric circuit is a(n):

A. Fuse

B. Conduit

C. Neutral core

D. Adapter

14. When buying an appliance on the installment plan, the fee you pay for borrowing money is known as the:

A. Contract

B. Purchase price

C. Interest

D. Down payment

15. Milk is low in:

A. Vitamin D

B. Calcium

C. Iron

D. Phosphorus

16. As a rule, fat in poultry:

A. Is distributed throughout the meat

B. Is found just under the skin

C. Is very low

D. Is fleshy

17. The inside temperature of a manual-defrost refrigerator:

A. Remains the same throughout the refrigerator

B. Has the warmest area at the bottom and door shelves

C. Has the coldest temperature in the middle shelf area

D. Has the warmest area on the top shelf

18. All of the following are true statements about the microwave oven EXCEPT:

A. It defrosts, reheats, and cooks foods rapidly

B. It cooks all foods in less time

C. Foods do not need to be cooked in additional water

D. It needs to be connected to a separate, grounded, 110-volt circuit

19. How many calories does a person need to cut in order to lose about half a kilogram (a pound) of weight a week?

   A. 300 calories a day

   B. 500 calories a day

   C. 700 calories a day

   D. 1000 calories a day

20. To prepare a conventional recipe in the microwave oven, you will need to reduce the cooking time for most recipes by about:

   A. 1/2

   B. 1/4

   C. 5 minutes

   D. 10 minutes

21. A buyer of goods and services is a:

   A. Supplier

   B. Manufacturer

   C. Consumer

   D. Manager

22. Cream with 18 to 30 percent milkfat is:

   A. Heavy cream

   B. Half-and-half

   C. Whipping cream

   D. Light, or coffee, cream

23. All of the following are true statements about kitchen safety and sanitation EXCEPT:

   A. Wear short sleeves or roll up long ones

   B. Wear disposable plastic gloves if you have an open cut on your hands

   C. Keep countertops, cookware, and floors clean

   D. Brush your hair back from your face with your hands while working with food

24. The number of servings daily from the milk group that 2- to 6-year- olds need is:

   A. 2 servingw

   B. 3 servings

   C. 4 servings

   D. 5 or more servings

25. **Aluminum cookware:**

    A. Conducts heat rapidly and evenly

    B. Does not darken or stain

    C. Can be put in a dishwasher

    D. Should not be scoured

26. **Which of the following contains NO cholesterol?**

    A. Foods of the animal origin

    B. Cells of the body

    C. Vegetable oil

    D. All of the above

27. **Heat that is transferred by direct contact is an example of:**

    A. Radiation

    B. Transaction

    C. Convection

    D. Conduction

28. **Foods that spoil easily are known as:**

    A. Imitation foods

    B. Perishable foods

    C. Fresh foods

    D. Processed foods

29. **When buying small appliances, look for all of the following EXCEPT:**

    A. Good balance

    B. Metal handles on heat-generating appliances

    C. UL seal on appliance, not just the cord

    D. Easy cleaning ability

30. **Most fresh vegetables should be used within:**

    A. 1 day

    B. 2 to 5 days

    C. 5 to 7 days

    D. 7 to 10 days

31. **An UNRELIABLE way to test the doneness of poultry is to:**

    A. Pierce with a fork

    B. Move the drumsticks gently

    C. Read the meat thermometer

    D. Check the color of the skin

32. **Security, enjoyment, self-esteem, and belonging are examples of:**

   A. Physical needs

   B. Emotional needs and desires

   C. Resources

   D. Social and cultural influences

33. **The single most important cause of kitchen accidents is:**

   A. Human carelessness

   B. Heavily trafficked areas

   C. Faulty equipment

   D. Improper clothing

34. **A practice that is considered essential to good table manners is:**

   A. Watching the actions of your host or hostess

   B. Blowing on hot food to cool it

   C. Tucking your napkin under your chin

   D. Breaking up food all at one time

35. **Chemical digestion begins in the:**

   A. Stomach

   B. Pancreas

   C. Small intestine

   D. Mouth

36. **The clues to managing meals successfully include:**

   A. Planning and making decisions

   B. Using the Daily Food Guide

   C. Using available resources

   D. All of the above

37. **Purchased salad dressings and mixes:**

   A. Are a poor substitute for home-prepared dressings

   B. Can save you many hours of preparation time

   C. Are less expensive than home-prepared

   D. Have a shorter shelf life

38. How long does the human body take to accept new behavior or eating habits?

   A. At least a week

   B. At least three weeks

   C. A minimum of two months

   D. One year or more

39. Liver, kidney, and heart are examples of:

   A. Choice meats

   B. Variety meats

   C. Select meats

   D. Prime meats

40. When buying kitchen equipment, you should do all of the following EXCEPT:

   A. Visit several stores to compare prices, quality, warranties, and special features

   B. Inquire about delivery and installation cost

   C. Analyze your family's needs as well as available space

   D. Choose the appliance that has the most special features

41. Overcooked meat is:

   A. Hard to digest

   B. Low in calories

   C. Very moist

   D. Tender

42. A type of salad green that has dark green, broad, curly leaves and a mild to bitter flavor is:

   A. Romaine lettuce

   B. Escarole

   C. Chinese cabbage

   D. Leaf lettuce

43. The illness that is not a type of food-borne illness is:

   A. Perfringen poisoning

   B. Appendicitis

   C. Salmonellosis

   D. Staphylococcal poisoning

**44. Overweight people are subject to all of the following problems EXCEPT:**

A. Such diseases as cancer and heart trouble

B. Strain on bones and muscles

C. Extra effort needed for breathing

D. Inability to perspire

**45. Carbohydrates that have been removed from their natural sources are called:**

A. Simple carbohydrates

B. Complex carbohydrates

C. Hidden carbohydrates

D. Processed carbohydrates

**46. The yield in a recipe refers to the:**

A. Unit cost per serving

B. Caloric weight of ingredients

C. Number of servings

D. Number of courses

**47. It is a safer and more efficient choice for a person confined to a wheelchair to have a:**

A. Freestanding range

B. Built-in oven and separate cooktop

C. Gas range

D. None of these

**48. When the demand for food is greater than the supply, prices tend to be:**

A. Lower

B. Higher

C. Similar

D. Fluctuating

**49. When buying pans, look for:**

A. Riveted handles

B. A matching set

C. Tight-fitting lids

D. Curved bottom

50. **The lunch that is the most balanced is:**

    A. Plain hamburger and milk

    B. Tomato soup, turkey sandwich and milk

    C. Macaroni and cheese, apple slices, and milk

    D. Grilled chicken, green beans, peaches, and ice water

51. **The most expensive and formal dinnerware is:**

    A. Earthenware

    B. China

    C. Melamine

    D. Stoneware

52. **All of the following statements relating to buying food are true EXCEPT:**

    A. Most convenience foods cost less than those made from scratch

    B. Unit pricing makes it easier to compare prices

    C. Price per serving is more important than price per pound

    D. Shoplifting increases the prices all consumers pay for products

53. **Properly wrapped poultry can be kept in the freezer for:**

    A. Several months

    B. Several weeks

    C. Up to one month

    D. About one year

54. **Green peppers, tomatoes, and raw cabbage are among the best sources of:**

    A. Vitamin A

    B. Thiamin

    C. Vitamin C

    D. Vitamin D

55. **Experts estimate that people in the United States waste at least:**

    A. One percent of edible food

    B. Five percent of edible food

    C. Ten percent of edible food

    D. Up to twenty percent of edible food

56. **The body's need for food is called:**

    A. Appetite

    B. Starvation

    C. Nutrition

    D. Hunger

**57. Money, skills, and imagination are examples of:**

A. Physical needs

B. Emotional needs and desires

C. Resources

D. Social and cultural influences

**58. Calories measure:**

A. Body weight

B. Fatness

C. Food energy

D. Basal metabolism

**59. Ground meats should be stored in the coldest part of the refrigerator and used:**

A. Within a week

B. Within 3 or 4 days

C. Within a day or two

D. Within 8 to 10 days

**60. To avoid curdling, milk should be:**

A. Cooked rapidly

B. Stirred constantly as it cooks

C. Mixed with an acid

D. Thickened with starch

**61. Which of the following is not a fat-soluble vitamin?**

A. Vitamin B

B. Vitamin A

C. Vitamin D

D. Vitamin E

**62. Foods that freeze well include:**

A. Potatoes and fresh fruit

B. Mayonnaise and custards

C. Poultry and bread

D. Lettuce and celery

**63. If foods in a microwave oven overcook, the:**

A. Power needs to be reduced

B. Food should be covered tightly

C. Food should be stirred

D. Food should be turned

**64. A dry-heat method for cooking poultry is:**

A. Braising

B. Stewing

C. Broiling

D. Simmering

**65. Most grains when overcooked become:**

A. Discolored

B. Hard

C. Sticky

D. Chewy

**66. Why are fruit juices better for you than carbonated drinks?**

A. Because they are high in sugar

B. Because they contain vitamins

C. Because they contain protein

D. Because they are higher in calories

**67. What is the name of the eating disorder that includes bingeing and self-induced vomiting?**

A. Anorexia nervosa

B. Peristalsis

C. Bulimia

D. Diabetes

**68. What best describes the U.S. RDA?**

A. A technical nutrient chart used mainly by health professionals

B. A simplified nutrient chart developed by the Food and Drug Administration (FDA)

C. A nutrient chart designed for persons under the age of 18

D. A nutrient chart designed for adults and the elderly

**69. In order to gain weight, a person should do which of the following:**

A. Choose higher-calorie foods from the food groups

B. Eat smaller meals five or six times a day

C. Exercise regularly

D. All of the above

**70. A low-power setting should be used for:**

A. Heating

B. Defrosting

C. Cooking

D. Browning

**71. Health experts recommend that of the calories you take in, fats should supply:**

A. 30 percent or less

B. 30 to 35 percent

C. 40 to 45 percent

D. 50 percent or more

**72. All of the following are types of sugar EXCEPT:**

A. Maltose

B. Laxtrose

C. Sucrose

D. Fructose

**73. In order to assist you when shopping, a shopping list should:**

A. Be arranged according to the layout of the store

B. Be alphabetical for easy use

C. Have your family's favorite food listed

D. Be limited in the number of items listed

**74. What may occur when a pregnant woman does not get enough calcium in her diet?**

A. Delivery of a blue-baby

B. Development of anemia

C. The taking of calcium from the mother's bones and teeth to supply the unborn baby

D. The placement of the baby on a calcium formula immediately after birth

**75. When does digestion begin?**

A. When food enters the stomach

B. As soon as a bite of food is taken into the mouth

C. When food enters the small intestine

D. When food enters the large Intestine

**76. Pasteurized milk:**

A. Improves the keeping quality

B. Changes the flavor

C. Allows the whey to be drained away

D. Decreases the amount of milkfat

77. **By law, sterling silver must contain:**

   A. 25.5 % silver

   B. 50.5 % silver

   C. 70.5 % silver

   D. 92.5 % silver

78. **A less tender class of poultry is a:**

   A. Roaster

   B. Stewing chicken

   C. Capon

   D. Broiler

79. **When buying tableware, you should first select:**

   A. Tablecloth and napkins

   B. Glassware

   C. Flatware

   D. Dinnerware

80. **The chief source of proteins in the vegan diet are:**

   A. Fruits and vegetables

   B. Milk and eggs

   C. Legumes and grains

   D. Chicken and turkey

81. **As people progress through their life cycle, their nutrient equirements:**

   A. Increase

   B. Remain the same

   C. Change

   D. Decrease

82. **The number of slices of bread from the Bread, Cereal, Rice, & Pasta Group that equal one serving is:**

   A. One slice

   B. Two slices

   C. Three slices

   D. Four slices

83. **A type of paint finish applied to kitchen walls because it washes more easily is:**

   A. Semi-gloss finish

   B. Flat finish

   C. Metallic finish

   D. Varnish finish

84. **When buying vegetables, choose ones that are:**

    A. Small

    B. Medium size

    C. Extra large

    D. Any size

85. **For dry storage, food should be stored:**

    A. Under the sink to save space

    B. Above the refrigerator or range

    C. In the lower drawer of a range

    D. In cool, dark areas away from moisture, light and heat

86. **Family traditions, advertising, current trends, and religious customs are examples of:**

    A. Physical needs

    B. Emotional needs and desires

    C. Resources

    D. Social and cultural influences

87. **To prevent the edges from turning brown, salad greens need to be:**

    A. Shredded

    B. Cut

    C. Diced

    D. Torn

88. **The best food sources of calcium are:**

    A. Meat, eggs, and beans

    B. Milk, cheese, and yogurt

    C. Oranges, grapefruit, and strawberries

    D. Whole grains

89. **The fork to be used first is placed:**

    A. To the right of the spoon

    B. To the right of the knife

    C. Farthest from the plate

    D. Closest to the plate

90. **When strong-flavored vegetables such as onions and cabbage are overcooked, the flavor becomes:**

    A. Bitter

    B. Sweet

    C. Milder

    D. Stronger

91. The use of alcohol and other drugs is linked with all of the following problems EXCEPT:

   A. Such medical problems as liver disease, cancer, and brain damage

   B. Loss of nutrients from the body

   C. Poor judgment and reactions

   D. Tendency to overeat

92. Salad ingredients should be drained to avoid:

   A. Bruising

   B. Wilting

   C. Diluting the salad dressing

   D. Spreading germs

93. When you diet, your first weight loss will consist of:

   A. Water

   B. Protein

   C. Sugars

   D. Fats

94. Skim milk has the following ingredient removed:

   A. Fat

   B. Calcium

   C. Protein

   D. Carbohydrates

95. Which of the following meals should be the largest meal of the day according to many health professionals?

   A. Breakfast meal

   B. Noon meal

   C. Evening meal

   D. Midmorning meal

96. When cooking fresh vegetables, the first step is always to:

   A. Boil water

   B. Wash the vegetables

   C. Cut them up

   D. Peel off skins

**97. The best way to choose the most reasonably priced food is to:**

A. Buy generic products

B. Compare unit pricing

C. Check nutrient value

D. Use coupons

**98. Purchased, pre-stuffed poultry should be:**

A. Thawed in the refrigerator

B. Cooked while still frozen

C. Thawed in cold water

D. Thawed in warm water

**99. Meats that have had some handling other than just cutting are called:**

A. Variety meats

B. Prime meats

C. Select meats

D. Processed meats

**100. If a warranty is called "limited":**

A. Its guarantee is for a shorter period of time than a full warranty

B. It has restrictions in addition to the time limit

C. It has not been UL approved

D. It covers only labor costs to the repair of the appliance

**101. An excellent example of nutrient teamwork is:**

A. Calcium and iron

B. Thiamin

C. Calcium and phosphorus

D. Folic acid

**102. The activity that uses more calories than the others is:**

A. Walking

B. Bowling

C. Dancing

D. Scrubbing

103. Four, sugar, and a blender should be stored in the:

A. Refrigerator-freezer center

B. Range center

C. Mixing center

D. Sink center

104. Foods that are canned, packaged, or frozen are best known as:

A. Enriched foods

B. Processed foods

C. Irradiated foods

D. Fortified foods

105. A knife most suitable for dividing cuts of meat is a:

A. Butcher knife

B. Boning knife

C. Utility knife

D. Chef's knife

106. When setting a table, the flatware should be arranged so the:

A. Knife is to the left of the plate

B. Forks are to the right of the plate

C. Piece you use first is farthest from the plate

D. Piece you use first is closest to the plate

107. The number of servings daily from the Vegetable Group that adults need is:

A. 1 serving

B. 2 servings

C. 3-5 servings

D. 6 servings or more

108. The number of servings daily of the Fruit Group that adults need is:

A. 1 serving

B. 2-3 servings

C. 2-4 servings

D. 3-5 servings

109. The number of servings daily of the Meat, Poultry, Fish, Dry Beans, Eggs, & Nuts Group that adults need is:

   A. 1-2 servings

   B. 2-3 servings

   C. 4 servings

   D. 5 servings or more

110. After shopping, the first foods to be stored at home should be:

   A. Meat and poultry

   B. Dairy products

   C. Frozen foods

   D. Produce

111. Vegetables cooked with butter, brown sugar, and water are called:

   A. Glazed

   B. Creamed

   C. Herbed

   D. Scalloped

112. The most expensive foods usually are:

   A. Dairy products

   B. Produce

   C. Grains and breads

   D. Meats

113. Keeping your weight the same is known as a:

   A. Seesaw diet

   B. Maintenance program

   C. Bulimia

   D. Fast

114. Suitable containers for microwaving include:

   A. Metal cookware and aluminum foil

   B. All plastic and glass-ceramic types

   C. Paper containers

   D. Containers that are not heat-resistant

115. **Stainless steel cookware:**

A. May darken if overheated

B. Heats quickly and evenly

C. May rust

D. Should not be scoured

116. **A food that can generally be cooked in a microwave is:**

A. An egg in the shell

B. French fries

C. A tuna casserole

D. All of these

117. **A system that allows computerized checkout counters to total the cost of a purchase is the:**

A. Standard of identity

B. Universal product code

C. Unit pricing

D. None of these

118. **The percent of your body weight that is composed of water is about:**

A. 10 %

B. 25 %

C. 65 %

D. 90 %

119. **A kitchen arrangement where appliances, storage cabinets, and counter space are in a ontinuous line is:**

A. A corridor

B. U-shaped

C. L-shaped

D. One-wall

120. **A pregnant woman's bones and teeth may be affected if her diet does not contain enough:**

A. Potassium

B. Iron

C. Calcium

D. Magnesium

121. **Salad dressing made with yogurt:**

A. Should not contain lemon or lime juice

B. Do not keep as well as other types

C. Are less nutritious than other dressings

D. Are lower in calories than other types

122. **A convection oven does NOT:**

A. Brown meats evenly

B. Cook food faster than a microwave

C. Maintain an even cooking temperature

D. Cook food faster than a conventional oven

123. **An average meal containing carbohydrates, proteins, and fats leaves the stomach in about:**

A. 2 hours

B. 4 hours

C. 1 hour

D. 24 hours

124. **Bread, potatoes, and macaroni are:**

A. Fatty foods

B. Starchy foods

C. Protein-rich

D. Diet foods

125. **When stir-frying vegetables, all of the following rules should be followed EXCEPT:**

A. Cut vegetables into small, uniform pieces

B. Use a small amount of oil

C. Begin cooking with most tender vegetables

D. Cover pan near end of cooking time

126. **The food most likely to be contaminated with salmonella bacteria is:**

A. Cooked spaghetti

B. Fresh poultry

C. Bread

D. Salad dressing

127. **Freezing temperatures cause most bacteria to:**

    A. Increase in number

    B. Decrease in number

    C. Stop multiplying

    D. Die off and disappear

128. **The Heimlich maneuver is used to help someone who:**

    A. Is choking

    B. Has a burn

    C. Has swallowed poison

    D. Has a severe cut

129. **The most tender cuts of meat come from the area of the animal that:**

    A. Gets the most movement

    B. Has well-developed muscle

    C. Is closest to the neck

    D. Is along the backbone

130. **All of the following are high in fat EXCEPT:**

    A. Margarine

    B. Whole milk

    C. Chocolate

    D. Fruits

131. **The costliest items of the amount spent on marketing food are:**

    A. Corporate profits

    B. Business taxes

    C. Advertising

    D. Labor and packaging

132. **In a microwave oven, food is cooked by:**

    A. Radon

    B. Magnetic attraction

    C. Friction

    D. Induction

133. **According to the Dietary Guidelines for Americans, you should do all of the following EXCEPT:**

    A. Avoid food with fiber

    B. Avoid excessive amounts of fat

    C. Avoid too much sugar

    D. Avoid too much sodium

134. **An Energy Guide label on a manual defrost refrigerator-freezer gives:**

    A. A description of the appliance and estimated yearly energy cost

    B. The number of times per year the unit must be defrosted

    C. The average temperatures of the refrigerator and the freezer

    D. A description of the warranty and manufacturer's guarantee

135. **A plan that makes use of space that might otherwise go unused in a large kitchen is the:**

    A. Island kitchen

    B. One-wall kitchen

    C. Basic kitchen

    D. L-shaped kitchen

136. **Of the following, the vegetable that is LOWEST in calories is:**

    A. Celery

    B. Corn

    C. Peas

    D. Potatoes

137. **It is important to scrub your hands immediately after all of the following EXCEPT:**

    A. Handling raw meat, poultry, fish, or eggs

    B. Coughing, sneezing, or touching your hair or face

    C. Playing with pets

    D. Chopping vegetables

138. **To remove food from liquid, you should use a:**

    A. Basting spoon

    B. Wooden spoon

    C. Slotted spoon

    D. Ladle

139. **A trash compactor would best be located at the:**

    A. Refrigerator-freezer center

    B. Range center

    C. Near kitchen exit

    D. Sink center

140. **Foods that take less time to cook in the microwave oven are:**

    A. Rice

    B. Macaroni

    C. Vegetables

    D. Pasta

141. **What may result from poor nutrition?**

    A. Overweight or underweight problems

    B. Skin problems

    C. Tooth decay

    D. All of the above

142. **A salad green with tender, deep green leaves and a sharp flavor is:**

    A. Leaf lettuce

    B. Fresh spinach

    C. Butter head lettuce

    D. Chinese cabbage

143. **How are foods divided into groups in the Food Guide Pyramid?**

    A. By the nutrients they contain

    B. By the number of servings recommended each day

    C. By the amount of calories in each food

    D. By the similarity in color

144. **Doneness of roasted meat is judged by:**

    A. Oven temperature

    B. Cooking method

    C. Texture

    D. Internal temperature

145. **A roasted bird is easier to carve if, after cooking, it stands for:**

    A. No additional time

    B. About 5 minutes

    C. About 15 minutes

    D. About 30 minutes

146. **Generic foods are:**

    A. Quality foods with brand names

    B. Quality foods without brand names

    C. Private labels for a specific store

    D. Unlabeled substandard products sold by manufacturers

147. **Buying open stock tableware means that:**

    A. Items are sold together as a set

    B. Items are usually less expensive than those sold differently

    C. Pieces can be added or replaced readily

    D. It is of inferior quality

148. **A small amount of exercise added to your activities can help speed up your metabolic rate and thereby decrease your:**

    A. Nervousness

    B. Energy

    C. Sleeplessness

    D. Set point

149. **Brown sugar is measured by:**

    A. Sifting it to remove any lumps

    B. Packing it into a cup until the sugar holds the cup's shape when inverted

    C. Spooning it into a cup and then shaking the cup firmly

    D. Spooning it loosely into a measuring cup

150. **To weigh your wants and needs and set goals, you use your:**

    A. Values

    B. Self-esteem

    C. Resources

    D. Instinct

**151.** **All of the following are true of exercise EXCEPT:**

A. It has emotional and physical benefits

B. It needs to be done a minimum of 7 hours per week

C. It improves flexibility

D. It conditions muscles

**152.** **Since athletes lose sodium and potassium through perspiration, what do they need to do?**

A. Take salt tablets and potassium supplements

B. Eat foods high in potassium

C. Avoid drinking water to slow down perspiration

D. Not make any adjustments since salt and potassium are present in most foods

**153.** **All of the following cookware materials are recommended for use in a microwave oven EXCEPT:**

A. Metal

B. Paper

C. Plastics

D. Ceramic

**154.** **An example of a water-soluble vitamin is:**

A. Vitamin A

B. Vitamin K

C. Vitamin C

D. Vitamin D

**155.** **Large, strong muscles are built by:**

A. Exercise

B. Extra amounts of protein

C. Extra amounts of water

D. Heredity

**156.** **How many servings of meat do 2- to 6-year olds need each day?**

A. 2 servings

B. 2-3 servings

C. 3-5 servings

D. 4 servings

**157.** **Pregnancy during adolescence presents special risks for:**

A. The baby

B. Both the mother and baby

C. The mother

D. None of the above

158. **The number of servings daily of the Fruit Group that 2- to 6-year olds need is:**

A. 1 serving

B. 2 servings

C. 2-3 servings

D. 3-5 servings

159. **Frozen poultry should be kept in its freezer wrapping and:**

A. Thawed on the counter

B. Thawed in hot water

C. Thawed in warm water

D. Thawed in the refrigerator

160. **People who are underweight should gain weight by:**

A. Choosing higher-calorie foods from the Daily Food Guide

B. Drinking a large soft drink before meals

C. Taking vitamin supplements

D. Exercising less and sleeping more

161. **Microwave energy is expressed in:**

A. Watts of electricity

B. Amperes of electricity

C. Power setting

D. Thermal units

162. **Cooking time in a microwave oven is affected by the:**

A. Amount of food

B. Shape of food

C. Original temperature of the food

D. All of these

163. **When buying iceberg lettuce, buy heads:**

A. That are tightly packed

B. That "give" slightly when squeezed gently

C. That have a large core

D. That are slightly over mature for milder flavor

164. A floor surface that is uncomfortable to stand on for a long period of time is:

A. Vinyl tile

B. Carpeting

C. Ceramic tile

D. Sheet vinyl

165. Salad greens should be:

A. Washed before they are stored

B. Washed and drained for several hours before they are stored

C. Stored without washing them first

D. Washed both before storing and before preparing

166. The energy the body needs to maintain basic processes is called:

A. Reproduction

B. Competition

C. Basal metabolism

D. Excretion

167. Food cooks more evenly in the microwave oven when it is placed in:

A. Round pans

B. Square pans

C. Rectangular pans

D. Plastic containers

168. The number of servings daily from the grain group that 2- to 6-year-olds need is:

A. 2 servings

B. 2-3 servings

C. 3-5 servings

D. 6 servings

**Answer Key**

| | | | | | | | |
|---|---|---|---|---|---|---|---|
| 1. | C | 44. | D | 89. | C | 134. | A |
| 2. | C | 45. | D | 90. | D | 135. | A |
| 3. | B | 46. | C | 91. | D | 136. | A |
| 4. | D | 47. | B | 92. | C | 137. | D |
| 5. | A | 48. | B | 93. | A | 138. | C |
| 6. | A | 49. | C | 94. | A | 139. | D |
| 7. | B | 50. | B | 95. | B | 140. | C |
| 8. | B | 51. | B | 96. | B | 141. | D |
| 9. | D | 52. | A | 97. | B | 142. | B |
| 10. | D | 53. | A | 98. | B | 143. | A |
| 11. | D | 54. | C | 99. | D | 144. | D |
| 12. | B | 55. | D | 100. | B | 145. | C |
| 13. | A | 56. | D | 101. | C | 146. | B |
| 14. | C | 57. | C | 102. | C | 147. | C |
| 15. | C | 58. | C | 103. | C | 148. | D |
| 16. | C | 59. | C | 104. | B | 149. | B |
| 17. | B | 60. | B | 105. | A | 150. | A |
| 18. | B | 61. | A | 106. | C | 151. | B |
| 19. | B | 62. | C | 107. | C | 152. | B |
| 20. | B | 63. | A | 108. | C | 153. | A |
| 21. | C | 64. | C | 109. | B | 154. | C |
| 22. | D | 65. | C | 110. | C | 155. | A |
| 23. | D | 66. | B | 111. | A | 156. | A |
| 24. | A | 67. | C | 112. | D | 157. | B |
| 25. | A | 68. | B | 113. | B | 158. | B |
| 26. | C | 69. | D | 114. | C | 159. | D |
| 27. | D | 70. | B | 115. | A | 160. | A |
| 28. | B | 71. | A | 116. | C | 161. | A |
| 29. | B | 72. | B | 117. | B | 162. | D |
| 30. | B | 73. | A | 118. | C | 163. | B |
| 31. | D | 74. | C | 119. | D | 164. | C |
| 32. | B | 75. | B | 120. | C | 165. | A |
| 33. | A | 76. | A | 121. | D | 166. | C |
| 34. | A | 77. | D | 122. | B | 167. | A |
| 35. | D | 78. | B | 123. | B | 168. | D |
| 36. | D | 79. | D | 124. | B | | |
| 37. | B | 80. | C | 125. | C | | |
| 38. | B | 81. | C | 126. | B | | |
| 39. | B | 82. | A | 127. | C | | |
| 40. | D | 83. | A | 128. | A | | |
| 41. | A | 84. | B | 129. | D | | |
| 42. | B | 85. | D | 130. | D | | |
| 43. | B | 86. | D | 131. | D | | |
| | | 87. | D | 132. | C | | |
| | | 88. | B | 133. | A | | |

"Are we there yet?"

"Gosh, now we've seen everything!"